The Balancing Act

Creating financial freedom
in the balance between
what you need and
what you have

Dave Baldwin

Published by Dave Baldwin Publishing in association with Hopeful Hill Press
All rights reserved. Printed in the United States of America.

First Edition
Cover art design: Dave Baldwin & Thomas Matthews

ISBN, Paperback   978-1-7336424-0-8
ISBN, eBook   978-1-7336424-1-5
Library of Congress Control Number: 2019903119

To buy additional copies please visit:
www.thebalancingactbook.com

For information, please contact:
Dave Baldwin
P.O. Box 4141, Carlsbad, CA 92018-4141
Email: Dave@thebalancingactbook.com

Acknowledgments:
Thank you to my good friend Bruce Rowe, who has helped transform pages upon pages of thoughts, notes and conversations into this book. Thank you to my sister Jennifer Burger for editing and pushing me across the finish line.

I dedicate this book to my wife Andrea. Thank you for believing in me, encouraging me, and supporting me through this project.

Table of Contents

Introduction

When I set out to write this book, I recognized my own past struggles with stress, financial pressure, and managing the balance between my lifestyle and my budget. Over the last decade, my career has put me in front of many people who are concerned about and struggle with some of those very same issues. These people have had a diverse range of backgrounds, income levels, and circumstances. No matter what those differences were, whether it was age, income or net worth, most people shared a few common themes:

- It is very easy to live at or above our means because we don't always understand exactly what our income is or what our lifestyle actually costs.
- We tend to overinflate our needs when justifying our lifestyle.
- Very few people have, and stick to, a plan that accounts for long-term goals when considering what their lifestyle should be in relationship to their means.

Those observations as well as my own experiences have allowed me to help others gain perspective and overcome the stress associated with these issues. I wanted to put down on paper the lessons I have learned as well as some reasons why we do what we do with respect to our spending and decisions around money.

I think we all recognize the obvious truth about money and stress. Not having enough money for the things that we need is stressful. Simple as that. We can further compound that feeling of stress by confusing our wants with our needs. Ultimately, being free from that stress—and achieving the feeling of financial freedom—is the result of having enough money to cover what we deem to be our needs.

In the end, creating financial freedom in the balance between what we need and what we have leaves only two options: make more or spend less. While making more is not always possible, the alternative of spending less tends to be an undesirable option. For some reading that last sentence, the thought of spending less brings on the very stress I am trying to help them avoid.

Most people don't want to take a step back, live on less, or give up the comforts they have grown accustomed to. We mistakenly think the idea of financial freedom means not having to follow a budget or account for how we spend our money. A lifestyle of limitations and balanced budgets can be stressful and probably feels like the exact opposite of financial freedom.

The rat race of chasing more income isn't much better for alleviating stress. The same challenges of living within our means exist at practically every level of income. The same desires, motivations, and justifications that allowed our lifestyles to meet our income and leave us feeling like the only solution is to make more money will follow us into our new income level.

When you consider the time and effort it takes to make more money, and that you could end up no better off with regard to the balance between your income and your needs, you may find that the only practical and sustainable solution is to spend less.

That's not to say you can't solve your problems through making more. Don't get me wrong—if you have the ability to make more, then go for it. Work hard and seek the income you deserve for your efforts. The stress of not being able to fulfill your needs may be the very motivating force that drives you to work harder and strive for more success.

The purpose of this book is to help you create financial freedom and making more money is one of your options. But if your goal is to reduce stress, then be careful trying to depend on increasing your income as the only way out of the hole.

You may find that the answer is a combination of both spending less and making more. But again, we have to be careful when finding our solution. We are problem solvers and we can find shortcuts or quick fixes to address our financial worries. Finding the right balance is a science, so to borrow a quote from theoretical physicist Richard Feynman, "The first principle is that you must not fool yourself, and you are the easiest person to fool."

The premise that financial freedom exists in the balance between what you need and what you have is easy to manipulate by not just looking to what you have, but instead looking at what you have *access to*. Using debt to bridge the gap and alleviate our stress is both easier than spending less and making more, and in the short term can be the path of least resistance.

There may be times when debt is the only way to afford something you need, like buying a house or a car. There may even be times when debt can be used as a strategy to leverage a position when buying something that can appreciate in value. What you should be wary of is the temptation to consume what you want today with tomorrow's money and get the immediate joy from that consumption without having to realize the immediate cost.

You may be dealing with the aftermath of this very temptation now. Addressing the ongoing costs of carrying your debt may also be the most significant way to reduce your spending and expand the margin between your lifestyle and income.

Again, I urge you to be careful in seeking quick fixes and shortcuts, as they can be just as detrimental to creating financial freedom as the bad habits that created the problem. If you have not committed to changes in spending, or if you have not addressed the mismatch between your lifestyle and your income, you may find yourself repeating your mistakes.

The big takeaway is that we are not alone. The challenge of managing our lifestyle and finding a sustainable balance between what we need and what we have is very common. It's something that not a lot of people feel completely comfortable talking about. Our friends, family, and peers could very well be going through different levels of stress and we might never know it.

There is no shortage of personal finance experts or resources to help guide people through the challenges of this difficult element of our lives. In fact, I've read through a lot of those resources along my personal journey and routinely lend these books out to my friends and clients.

I wrote this book because I want to make myself available to help people overcome this struggle. I want to address *why* we experience financial stress, *why* we are driven to live right up to the limit of our means, and *how* we can be empowered to solve the problem. This book is my way of sharing what I've discovered about overcoming financial stress and finding financial freedom. The sooner you can figure this out, the longer you can experience the benefits.

1: Financial Freedom

*"It's the good advice that you just didn't
take. Who would've thought... it figures"*
—Alanis Morrissette and Glen Ballard, ©1995,
Maverick Records

Remember the '90s song "Ironic" by Alanis Morrissette? It was a long list of situations that didn't work out the way they were supposed to. Whether you chalk it up to bad luck or poor timing, it is certainly frustrating when everything seems to be going wrong. Perhaps they should have called the song "Frustrating" instead, although that probably wouldn't have been as catchy.

If you're reading this book, getting your personal finances on track and reducing financial stress in your life may be a source of frustration. You may have tried over and over to make very simple changes in your spending habits and it just hasn't taken hold. The world entices you to spend or an unexpected expense pops up, derailing your best efforts.

This book is aimed at helping you overcome that frustration. It will provide you with an understanding of why you spend your dollars the way you do and show you how to implement a plan to achieve what you want.

Time to write a new script

Your life may keep taking turns like a movie plot, where a simple objective gets foiled by the least likely obstacle, dragging out the story and creating doubt that the characters will be successful in their endeavor.

Classic comedies like "Planes, Trains, and Automobiles" or any of the infamous "Vacation" adventures of Clark Griswold might come to mind. While the frustrating turns of events in those movies elicit cheap laughs, you probably don't feel like laughing when it comes to your finances.

The graphic below outlines a typical screenplay plotline:

Stage 1 Setup	Stage 2 New Situation	Stage 3 Progress	Stage 4 Complications	Stage 5 Final Push	Stage 6 Aftermath
Turning Point #1 Opportunity	Turning Point #2 Change of Plans	Turning Point #3 Point of no Return	Turning Point #4 Major Setback	Turning Point #5 Climax	
Act 1		Act 2		Act 3	

Figure 1.1

The first act introduces the "hero" of our story and an opportunity is presented. Characters develop in the setup stage and more information about the situation becomes clear. Success will be difficult. It will require commitment and a more serious approach than first thought. This change of plans shifts the story into Act Two.

In the third and fourth stages there is progress, but complications present higher stakes and the hero reaches a point of no return. A major setback or a chance of failure moves our story into Act Three. Then in a final push—the climax—our hero accomplishes his or her goal.

Viewing those plot turning points in terms of personal finance aspirations, I think you'll see a journey that can be surprisingly similar to finding your path to financial freedom:

- **Opportunity**: The vision of a life without financial stress. A desire to be free from the burden of debt or the rat race of chasing after more money.

- **Change of Plans**: Learning the challenges you face, you know that bad habits will be hard to break. Transforming your lifestyle to align with your desire for financial freedom will take sacrifice and difficult choices. Your old ways must change.

- **Point of No Return**: Permanent changes are made and goals are set. The commitment to change eliminates the opportunity to turn back.
- **Major Setback**: Challenges may present a feeling that you can't do it. The task at hand seems too hard. Temptations threaten to prevent achievement of the ultimate goal.
- **Climax**: Success! The ability to persevere and overcome your challenges has revealed a new and better life, free from financial worry.

Perhaps you are starting to see *your* opportunity and a vision for financial freedom. The challenge of rewriting your financial script is probably not as difficult as you imagine, but only if you focus ahead to the long-term satisfaction you'll feel in achieving goals that are most important to you. Let's explore what that can mean for you and your lifestyle.

What is financial freedom?

According to the "Stress in America" survey conducted annually by the American Psychology Association, money is consistently one of the top causes of stress for Americans, and it has been since this survey began in 2007. The idea of financial freedom is minimizing—or even eliminating—financial stress. It's freedom from the worries of not having enough money for the things you want or need. It's ending the constant struggle and the rat race to have more.

It doesn't mean you have to be a minimalist, or that you shouldn't be willing to work hard for life's rewards. But what good is working 60-plus hours a week to afford a lifestyle that you're too busy to enjoy? It's like selling your car for gas money or exercising to the point of injury. It defeats the purpose.

It's easy to overinflate the amount of hard work it takes to achieve success and, in turn, magnify the reward we think we deserve for that hard work. This justification for spending, especially if it leads to overspending, can create a compounding deficit that requires more earnings to pay for that reward.

Instead, it's about being content with what you have and *balancing* what you want with what it takes to achieve it.

The Well-Being Index and the benefits of living below your means

The objective of this book is to show you how to limit your needs to something less than what you can afford. Put another way—to live below your means. Then, to the degree that you can create a *margin* between what you earn and what you spend, you can experience a true freedom from financial stress.

Rather than "threaten" you into changing your financial habits with negative statistics about the potential for stress, let's focus on the positive benefits you can bring to your life. Some interesting research has found that your overall well-being is directly influenced by your financial well-being.

The "State of American Well-Being"[1] study uses data collected as part of the Gallup-Healthways Well-Being Index. The data is distilled from 176,702 interviews across all 50 states. As the study states:

> "Financial well-being is an often-overlooked determinant of overall health, medical costs and workplace performance. Consequently, improving financial well-being is important for employers, health plans and other population health stakeholders.
>
> Additionally, people who are thriving in financial well-being also tend to have higher thriving rates in purpose, social and community well-being; better physical health; and better outcomes in other key well-being items. Those

with high financial well-being are less likely to have depression, diabetes, high blood pressure, and obesity. They are also more likely to engage in healthy behaviors such as exercise, eating fresh produce, and not smoking; and are more likely to feel active and productive every day, like what they do, learn or do something interesting every day, and get positive energy from friends and family."

Maybe it's not a new diet or more caffeine you need after all. The study shows that when you gain financial freedom, you'll boost satisfaction and performance in nearly a dozen areas of your life, including your relationships, health, and mood.

More results from the Gallup-Healthways study show that only a little better than a third of us were found to be "thriving" in financial well-being:

"In 2014, only 39 percent of the country was thriving in financial well-being; with a majority of Americans (61 percent) struggling or suffering in this element. Although financial well-being does get better with age, and also with higher income, being a high earner doesn't always ensure higher financial well-being. Of those earning more than $120,000 per year, 43% are still struggling or suffering in financial well-being in 2014."

Obviously, it is possible to live comfortably at many levels of income because someone out there is doing it. Envying the "next guy up" on the pay scale is as old as time. But we prosper when we develop a mindset of "this is what I have and this is what I can spend," and come to appreciate the control and choices that come our way in the form of discretionary dollars when there is a margin between our income and our needs.

If you can look at what's driving you to spend at the level you do and why it is difficult to live within your means, then you can address that and fix the problem. This book can help you identify ways to live below your means so that you can provide yourself with a new level of financial contentment and security.

With continued discipline to live below your means, you can grow your wealth with the amount saved. Then, with more wealth, you can either *sustainably* increase your lifestyle or further reduce financial stress.

It's not about more income

We often think "If I just had a little more per month, then I would have all that I *need*." But thinking *more* is the answer is not likely to lead you to financial freedom. (In fact, this is a quick way to diagnose how much you are probably overspending.)

A study by psychologist Daniel Kahneman and economist Angus Deaton titled "High income improves evaluation of life but not emotional well-being" found that we quickly adapt to rises in income:

> "Because of *adaptation*, the difference in well-being between two random individuals whose income differs by $100,000 is far less impressive than the joy and misery that these individuals would immediately experience were they to trade places.
>
> In the present study, we confirm the contribution of higher income to improving individuals' life evaluation, even among those who are already well off. However, we also find that the effects of income on the emotional dimension of well-being satiate fully at an annual income of approximately $75,000…Beyond ~$75,000 in the contemporary United States, however, higher income is neither the road to experience happiness nor the road to the relief of unhappiness or stress…"

This concept, known as hedonic adaptation or the "hedonic treadmill," is when we chase the thought that "just a little bit more" will bring us contentment and financial stability. But a number of studies, including work by Kahneman and behavioral economics professor Dan Ariely, have confirmed what you have probably experienced: The emotional lift we gain with a salary increase or new purchase quickly dissipates. Then onward we go, setting our sights ahead to find another rush from the next one.

I know this all too well from my own personal story. Despite consistently increasing my income year after year for a decade, I didn't reduce my stress—I added to it. With each increase, I just increased my lifestyle and spending to match.

Also, there may have been a time when it was common to lock into a career and expect higher and higher earnings until we retire, but that is simply not the case today. The more typical career path is one with income ups and downs, along with periods of transition with no income at all.

PayScale Inc.[3] collects income data and helps its clients ensure that they pay the right wages for their employees based on factors such as years of experience, location, education level, etc. The company has collected data that shows men's wage increases peak at age 48 and women's income at age 39. At that point, the data showed some—but much smaller— wage increases that probably aren't even enough to keep up with inflation.

It's not hoping for a windfall

Many of us have had the idea that we could "win the lottery." Maybe not an actual lottery, since the odds are stacked so high, but to experience some event that drops a windfall of money in our lap.

Perhaps the dot-com excitement of the late '90s or the run up in housing prices of the mid-2000s lured you into investments that seemed to promise an easy payoff. Or, if you followed the cryptocurrency phenomenon and the meteoric rise of Bitcoin in 2017, you may have been tempted to join in the excitement.

Stories of people making their fortunes—seemingly overnight—investing in the "next big thing" are not new. Whether it's from the past few decades or the mid-1800s California gold rush, the excitement of these get-rich-quick narratives have the power to attract our attention and affect our behavior. We want to believe that it could have been us— that we might just catch that same stroke of luck and solve all our financial problems.

But the odds that we're uniquely talented at picking the next big thing are small, and most likely inflated based on how our human psyche really works. Optimism and overconfidence can lead us to believe that if somebody else did it, it's also possible for us to have a similar experience.

We naturally tend towards a feeling of irrational overconfidence in our minds. An example is a 1981 study by researcher Ola Sverin titled "Are we all less risky and more skillful than our fellow drivers?", which found that when participants were asked how they rated their driving ability relative to other drivers, close to 80 percent felt they were safer than the average driver. The little problem here is that based on what a mathematical average is, no more than 50 percent could *actually* be average or better.

State lotteries routinely see an uptick in the number of tickets sold when the jackpot reaches a larger than average payout. Even though the odds don't change, people become interested in playing when the winnings are at a greater level. You may even feel the desire to purchase multiple tickets to "increase your chances" of winning. The logical fallacy in this thinking is that while one lottery ticket may have a 1 in 300 million chance of winning, "doubling your odds" by purchasing a second ticket is still statistically insignificant.

Now indeed, there are those who have made their fortune in a variety of speculative investments, and there are those who were just plain lucky. These examples make it tempting to think about a windfall coming our way. But that's not a realistic strategy to gain financial freedom.

Identifying your sources of financial stress

It's human nature to constantly strive for more, and something that is programmed into us from an early age. But it should be clear now that if your financial plan is to just keep earning more, you'll likely adjust your spending to any increase and potentially mismanage the income from your peak earning years. You may look back with regret that you didn't put that money to better uses for you or your family's future and your financial stress will most likely continue to grow, rather than be reduced.

And that points out the biggest flaw in the "more income fix": It doesn't get at the underlying motivations behind your spending. We've all heard about people who actually do win a lottery, or entrepreneurs and professional athletes who briefly earn lottery-esque money, and then fall back to financial rock bottom.

Instead, we need to reprogram our habits to overcome this cycle.

The first step forward is to look into our lives and learn what gives us financial stress. The following is a self-assessment that will help you discover sources of financial stress as well as how that financial stress is spilling over into other areas of your life.

To better understand your individual situation, complete this exercise now. This is a good first step in preparing to make the changes recommended in the following chapters and finding your financial freedom.

Financial Self-Assessment

1. In terms of managing your personal finances, would you rate your skills below average, average, or above average?
2. Do you feel satisfied with the lifestyle your current income provides?
3. What additional amount of monthly income do you think would provide what you need and eliminate financial stress from your life?
4. Reviewing the past five years, in how many of those years have you increased your income?
5. What did you do with your last bonus, tax refund or unexpected income?
6. Is income the primary reason for staying in your job?
7. If you didn't have to "work for a living," what would you really like to do instead?
8. If you lost your job, could you pay all your bills for six months?
9. Do you track what you spend each month? If so, What are your total monthly expenses?
10. How many credit cards or lines of credit (home equity, auto, retail) do you have?
11. What is your total debt from all sources, not including your mortgage?
12. Do you know how much you need to save for retirement? Are you saving enough?
13. If you are planning to help pay for your children to go to college, do you know how much you need to save? Are you saving enough?
14. Would you say your spending decisions are more impulsive or part of a plan?

15. What were the top five factors you considered when choosing the last vehicle you purchased? List factors like safety, luxury, prestige, economy, budget, etc. from highest priority to lowest.

16. Are big-picture impacts—e.g., environmental impact, food sustainability, children's future—important to you in your consumption and spending choices? Be specific in listing your priorities.

17. When it comes to purchase decisions, would you say you trust your gut or are more reasoned in how you decide?

18. Are you a "sale" shopper who is good at getting great deals on what you buy?

19. Do you believe that higher-priced products are usually better?

20. Do you like to keep up with the latest trends in your consumption and spending choices?

21. How often do you have regrets after a purchase?

22. Can you remember a purchase you thought would make you happy but instead caused you financial stress?

23. Do you often experience thoughts of stress or feelings of being overwhelmed by your financial situation?

24. Why haven't you made changes in your spending and/or savings habits to this point?

25. If your finances are shared with a spouse or partner, do you agree on most or all expenses? If you have money disagreements, are they affecting your relationship?

26. Are there any other ways that financial stress might be affecting your lifestyle and/or relationships? Be specific.

If you manage your budget with a spouse or partner, there is one more budgeting behavior that is often a major source of financial stress. Some people hide expenses or money from the people they share their finances with.

Obviously, hiding the truth isn't healthy, and what's more, it's going to prevent you from growing in how you make your spending decisions. The following questions may help to get you on the same page with the person you are managing your budget with.

27. Regardless of your reason, have you ever hidden a purchase or secretly put money aside without your spouse or partner's knowledge?
28. Why did you feel like you needed to hide this?
29. Do you think separating your finances or setting aside money of your own each month would improve the situation or not? Why?
30. Do you and your financial partner share common financial goals? Do your actions of hiding money or purchases undermine those goals?
31. What discussion could you have with your spouse or partner to better understand both your individual and your shared financial goals? How can you work together to achieving those goals as partners?

Having completed your self-assessment, the sources of financial stress in your life should be coming into focus.

Next, we look at what drives the money-stress connection and how that affects our financial decisions.

Chapter Notes

1) "State of American Well-Being," 2014 Financial Well-Being Rankings, Gallup-Healthways Well-Being Index

2) "High income improves evaluation of life but not emotional well-being," Daniel Kahneman and Angus Deaton, Proceedings of the National Academy of Sciences of the United States of America, September 21, 2010

3) Gender Lifetime Earnings Gap, Infographic, PayScale Inc., https://www.payscale.com/gender-lifetime-earnings-gap#methodology

2: Why We Feel Stress About Money

*"If you don't know where you're going,
you'll end up someplace else."*
—*Yogi Berra, Major League
Baseball Hall of Fame*

Financial stress is the result of either not having enough money to meet your needs or feeling forced to earn more to satisfy them. The source of that stress comes from the mismatch between where you are financially and where you would like to be.

The path toward financial freedom will be challenging. Just like in our movie plot, there will be turning points and obstacles to keep you from reaching your goals.

When we understand our natural responses to the mismatch between what we need and what we have, then we can gain more control. When we understand our motivations to spend and what drives us to consume, then we can make better choices that lead us toward our goals, rather than getting derailed or knocked off course.

Maslow's Hierarchy of Needs

To better understand these concepts, let's look at Maslow's Hierarchy of Needs. This well-known idea was proposed by psychologist Abraham Maslow in his paper "A Theory of Human Motivation," published in 1943 in *Psychological Review*.

Maslow gives us a simple framework to help us identify what our needs truly are, and where they come from.

The central premise is that all humans have a set of needs that must be met to achieve their full potential. Represented as a pyramid (shown below), the hierarchy starts with basic needs like food, water, and shelter. As those needs are achieved, we move on to fulfill higher levels of needs like safety, social belonging, and esteem. Maslow believed our actions are driven by the motivation to fulfill these needs and that when all of our needs are met, we can reach our full potential or "self-actualization."

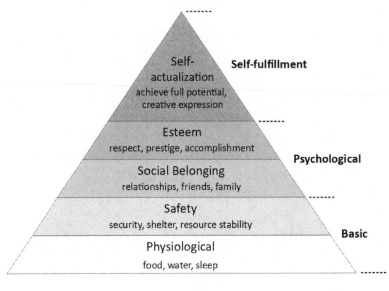

Figure 2.1

Basic needs – physiological and safety

We need food, water, and sleep to live and, until we satisfy those needs, we don't tend to worry about much more. If you're reading this book you are likely able to provide yourself these necessities. Depending on how steady your income stream is, you are also probably able to provide them on a fairly consistent basis, which ultimately meets your safety and security needs as well.

It will inevitably be your priority to spend the first dollar you make to fulfill your basic needs. Since you naturally place a priority on addressing hunger, you probably apply little thought toward those purchases. The cost of any one meal is small relative to the total amount of money you have available.

When it comes to buying a week's worth of groceries or a more expensive restaurant meal, you may be more aware of the cost relative to what you have, but you are still likely to prioritize these expenses over other needs.

Other expenses that fall into this basket of basic needs, like household bills and utilities, are sometimes harder to track because of billing cycles or the way we pay for them. How much will it cost to keep the heater turned up just a little higher in the winter, take a longer shower, or repeat a dryer cycle to get the wrinkles out of a forgotten load of laundry? We know that there is a cost, but we are not immediately faced with the actual cost and we're hardwired to place a priority on these necessities.

But consider the feeling of stress you may experience if an unexpected change to your income threatens your ability to provide these basic needs. Also consider the magnification of that stress if you have an obligation to provide for a family. Perhaps you have experienced the loss of a job or cut in salary and know firsthand this kind of stress.

While having a steady and adequate income will certainly help you fulfill safety through resource stability, it's not a guarantee. If you work in commissioned sales or in a trade where pay can change with your hours or workload, your income may be unpredictable. In that case, you are probably well aware of the stress that can come with the ups and downs of your paycheck.

Maybe an unexpected expense threatens your ability to provide the *same level* of necessities that you or your family are accustomed to. The Federal Reserve System "2016 Report on the Economic Well-Being of U.S. Households"[1] found that 44 percent of households would be unable to come up with $400 for an emergency expense and would need to either borrow the money or sell something to cover it.

It doesn't even need to be an unexpected expense. It could be just a slight oversight on spending, a spontaneous purchase, or a one-time splurge that puts you over the top, requiring you to wait until payday to make your normal grocery run. While not at the same level as losing a job, these are stressful situations, well-known to many of us, and rooted in our need to consistently provide the basic necessities for ourselves or our family.

Psychological needs – belonging, love, and esteem

People have a natural desire for social belonging. We want to interact with others, build relationships, and maintain friendships. Whether single or married with children, we want to feel like we belong and fit in.

You might have a social job where interaction needs are met while you earn an income, but most likely you'll have to spend some money to socialize. We might have friends who like getting together informally, without a need to spend a lot of money just to be together. On the other hand, we might have expensive hobbies that enable us to socialize with others who share the same interests. Depending on who you spend your time with and what you do for fun, that can be expensive.

We tend to socialize with people of the same socioeconomic status, with similar homes, cars, lifestyles, and discretionary expenses. Not only do you have to contend with satisfying this need and the costs you may incur, but you're more likely to feel pressure to keep up. When you try to "keep up with the Joneses" and find these activities pushing you beyond your means, the pressure adds up to more stress.

Beyond just fitting in socially with others, the need to belong can drive you toward intimate relationships, a desire to partner with someone else, and perhaps raise a family. Partnering with someone may be a very efficient way to go through life and could be a great benefit, emotionally and financially. With no children—either by choice or circumstances—you could earn the title of DINK (Dual Income, No Kids) or DINKER (Dual Income, No Kids, Early Retirement).

Please don't take this as a recommendation to avoid having kids so you can enjoy an early retirement, but it could be part of your long-term planning considerations. As a parent, I can personally attest to the emotional benefit of raising children, but it is not without cost *and stress.*

The "Expenditures of Children by Families, 2015"[2] report (U.S. Department of Agriculture) tracks the average annual cost of raising a child and it currently sits at $12,980 per year, or $284,570 to raise a child to the age of 18 with projected inflation factored in. And, as you can see, this figure doesn't consider the cost of college.

Whether you are trying to fit in with others or providing for a family to meet your social belonging needs, there are lifestyle expenses involved. Just as we recognize the stress of not being able to meet our basic needs, we can experience additional stress from our need for social belonging.

Esteem needs – respect, prestige, and accomplishment

Once we satisfy the sense of social belonging, we seek to fill our need for esteem and respect. Much like the social-belonging stage, where we begin to look at how others see us to fit in, esteem needs enter the picture and magnify this desire.

This aspiration goes beyond wearing the right clothes, driving the right car, or living in the right neighborhood. We want to compare ourselves to others and derive our self-worth from how our lifestyles match up. This is where spending can easily exceed income and you begin to understand how lifestyle choices can lead to stress. Again, if the basic needs, safety and security needs, or social belonging needs are not met, these esteem needs will probably be of little concern.

Maslow thought of this need as split into two components: a "lower" need to get respect, status and recognition from others, and a "higher" need for self-respect and self-esteem.

The higher esteem needs can be very difficult to satisfy for some. It's not something you can simply buy more of or adjust your budget to attain. Self-esteem, as the Merriam-Webster dictionary defines it, is "a confidence and satisfaction in oneself, or a feeling of having respect for yourself and your abilities." Those abilities, characteristics, or attributes can cover any number of categories, from personality and intelligence, to physical strength and appearance, or even academic or vocational achievements.

If you feel a natural satisfaction with yourself and your abilities, this may be a component of your life where you can simply check the box. Or you may be driven to make up for what you *perceive* to be personal shortfalls by splurging on material items or activities that artificially boost your self-confidence or esteem.

In the absence of self-esteem, some may place an emphasis on what Maslow referred to as the "lower esteem need" or respect and recognition from others. Who doesn't enjoy the feeling of accomplishment and its associated prestige? Despite the negative association with the term "lower esteem need," this can be a positive motivator to encourage you to work hard to gain recognition from others and doesn't always equate to spending money on something just to impress people.

However, filling your esteem needs can absolutely be a cause of overspending. Think of a time when you spent money on something that you thought would get you recognition or boost your self-esteem only to find that feeling fade. The phrase "money can't buy you happiness" certainly applies here.

The idea that money can be used to fulfill needs goes all the way back to our most innate desire to provide food, water, and shelter. But as we make the association between money and our ability to fulfill our needs, we open ourselves to mismanaging our financial resources. We may place too much emphasis on fulfilling our esteem or social belonging needs and in doing so risk the ability to fulfill other needs by spending money we don't have and taking on debt.

If spending money doesn't build your self-esteem, could overspending worsen it? Consider the results of mismanaging your finances and the negative feelings that could generate. Now consider the benefits of managing your finances appropriately. Would the confidence of knowing you're doing a good job controlling your spending provide a *real* boost to your self-esteem?

The Drum Major Instinct

It's also this lower esteem need, or desire for recognition, that marketers routinely target as a way to appeal to our consumption desires. A recent Superbowl commercial for a pickup truck used audio from a Dr. Martin Luther King Jr. sermon titled "The Drum Major Instinct." It stands out as an interesting example. In this sermon Dr. King describes greatness as a willingness to serve and the commercial highlighted that this brand of pickup truck was built to serve.

In a broader theme in his sermon, Dr. King spoke about our ego and desire to be recognized. Our natural craving for attention starts with our very first cry as a baby. He described an urge to be regarded as great, to be above others, to be out front like a drum major in a parade.

This same craving for attention can extend to living beyond our means and comparing ourselves to our neighbors.

It's ironic that the sermon, in which Dr. King urged us not to fall for marketers trying to appeal to our ego, is used for marketing purposes. In fact, Dr. King *specifically* called out auto manufacturers for doing just that.

Many of our challenges in deciphering between needs and wants will inevitably circle back to this concept of ego. How many of our decisions to spend money are to fulfill our esteem needs? And further, how many of our decisions are being influenced by outside sources?

Wants vs needs

Maslow's theory suggests that we can't do much about our innate desire to fulfill our needs. However, if we can isolate the "needs" from the "wants" then we can limit the money required. With a smaller bucket to fill, we can shed stress from our lives.

The positive benefits of a balanced life can also be compared to Maslow's highest need of self-actualization. We want balance. We want to achieve our full potential. With a truthful assessment of needs versus wants, we can knock down some obstacles on our path to financial freedom.

Ask yourself, what really is *enough* food, water, and shelter? While grocery shopping, how often do you buy the expensive brand rather than the sale or better value items?

Even our choice of stores (the nice, new one versus the more economical) might deserve a closer look. You need to understand the choices you make even at this basic level, so you are empowered to manage or change them to reduce financial stress.

The stress connection

It should be clear by now that the connection between money and our ability to fulfill our needs, along with the connection between unfulfilled needs and stress, draws a direct link between money and stress. When money equals fulfilled needs, and money becomes scarce, then unfulfilled needs become sources of stress. Put simply: not having enough money is stressful.

Even though Abraham Maslow wrote his theory in 1943, he is well-known for his significant contributions to modern psychology. While his hierarchy was not specifically written to explain the relationship between unfulfilled needs and stress, it is easy to infer. But let's consider more recent contributions to behavioral psychology and a more direct connection between stress and meeting our needs.

Scarcity – stress reduces impulse control

In this book's introduction, I briefly discussed the stress that comes from your needs exceeding your resources. This obvious truth about stress and not having enough money for the things that you need is explained by behavioral scientist and Princeton professor Eldar Shafir in his 2014 book, *Scarcity: The New Science of Having Less and How It Defines Our Lives*, co-authored with economist and Harvard economics professor Sendhil Mullainathan.

Dieters are familiar with the feelings that come with depriving yourself of something you really want (or even need). Your mind begins to obsess about what is now otherwise unavailable. You think about how good dessert tastes, or the satisfaction that comes from eating until you are completely full. You might even reevaluate why you're dieting in the first place.

That obsession is a natural response, almost a survival strategy your mind uses to cope with your situation. Shafir and Mullainathan describe it as a frame of mind:

> "When we experience scarcity of any kind, we become absorbed by it. The mind orients automatically, powerfully, toward unfulfilled needs. For the hungry, that need is food. For the busy it might be a project that needs to be finished. For the cash-strapped it might be this month's rent payment; for the lonely, a lack of companionship. Scarcity is more than just the displeasure of having very little. It changes how we think. It imposes itself on our minds."

This singular focus can be beneficial. Your mind sets your priority and is actively preventing anything else from disrupting your ability to fulfill this otherwise unfulfilled need. If you've felt the pressure of a rapidly-approaching deadline, you may have miraculously found the focus to overcome procrastination, avoid distraction, and finish your project. This is the result of your mind coping with the scarcity of time.

However, this attention can also have a very negative affect. As your focus is narrowed to the highest priority item, you may lose focus on more peripheral issues that can quickly magnify if not addressed.

This effect is described by Shafir and Mullainathan as "tunneling" and is very applicable to how we cope with financial stress. It also sets the stage for how much stress we're able to deal with at any given time. This so-called "bandwidth" that Mullainathan and Shafir describe in their book "measures our computational capacity, our ability to pay attention, to make good decisions, to stick with our plans, and to resist temptations. Bandwidth correlates with everything from intelligence and SAT performance to impulse control and success on diets."

Social experiment – the proof is in the (sugary) pudding

In their book, Shafir and Mullainathan describe an experiment in which they worked with sugarcane farmers in India to test the effects of financial stress on their ability to perform mentally. Sugarcane farmers typically make the majority of their yearly income from their crops at harvest time, leaving them income to live the rest of the year.

Shafir and Mullainathan chose this group as subjects to isolate the mental performance under financial stress. The farmers were first given IQ tests prior to harvest when last year's take was running low, then again after the harvest when the farmers received their big payday and the research showed interesting results. The farmers scored higher on average after the harvest when financial stress was minimal.

In another experiment, the researchers looked at the effect that stress had on impulse control. They tested the response to stress by giving people a mental task of remembering a set of numbers. Some people were asked to remember a two-digit while others were asked to remember a seven-digit number. The subjects then waited in a lobby before being called back to recall the numbers they were asked to remember.

In the lobby, an assortment of cake and fruit was available to both groups of test subjects. The resulting choices were telling. The group burdened with the harder task of remembering a seven-digit string of numbers ate cake 50 percent more often than the group asked to remember the simpler string of only two numbers. The test subjects were not dieting and had no way of knowing that the cake or fruit choice was even part of the experiment. But their natural resistance to the impulsive desire to eat cake dissipated with the stress of having to remember a longer string of numbers.

This experiment and other similar research strongly indicate that when your mind is preoccupied by some other burden it is less likely to effectively manage impulse control.

Negative feedback loops – stress multiplies stress

A "feedback loop" is when the output of a system is tied back to the input so the system itself is affected along with its output. If the result is positive, like success begetting more success, that's a positive feedback loop. On the other hand, if the loop output was stress from making poor financial decisions feeding back into a system of more stress, followed by more poor decisions, followed by more stress, this ever-repeating, downward spiral is a negative feedback loop.

We depend on our cognitive intelligence to make good decisions and the stress of unfulfilled needs directly hinders our ability to make these decisions. The consequence for this can very easily lead to a negative feedback loop.

Consider the well-being index discussed in Chapter 1. Financial stress has a negative impact on many other areas of our lives. If stress can affect our willpower or impair our ability to make the best, healthiest, most strategic, or beneficial decisions, then any imbalance in our life that results in stress can kick off a negative feedback loop that includes the consequence of unfulfilled needs and financial stress.

We all share a basic set of human needs. When they go unfulfilled, we feel stress. While Maslow's Hierarchy of Needs gives us a rational framework to understand that relationship, our complicated minds also work against us. Even without the cognitive limitations brought on by stress, making financial decisions is really, really hard simply because of our human nature. In the next chapter, we'll learn more about our irrational side, how that affects the way we think about money, and how to be more aware of the effects so we can make better decisions.

Chapter Notes

1) "2016 Report on the Economic Well-Being of U.S. Households," The Federal Reserve System, May 2017

2) "Expenditures of Children by Families, 2015," U.S. Department of Agriculture, January 2015

3: Getting to Know the Irrational Self

"Humans are hard-wired to be irrational when it comes to financial decisions. We must understand that so we don't become the sucker at the poker table."
——*Whitney Tilson, investor, author, philanthropist*

Economists have historically given too much credit to human behavior and our ability to act rationally. Economic policies are mostly based on the assumption that we will act in our best interest, make good decisions, and spend money in ways that make sense.

You'll see this in action when governments and central banks raise and lower interest rates—the cost of money—to spur consumer spending or slow inflation. While these economic practices have proven effective in influencing human behavior, the models predict our response based on presumptions that we will act rationally.

Consider the housing market in 2005 and 2006. Historically low interest rates clearly encouraged consumers to buy homes. What economic models failed to predict was that a large number of those consumers would buy homes they couldn't really afford, with interest-only, negative-amortization, minimum-payment loans.

This lack of rational behavior goes far beyond the consumer. The mortgage and banking industries were complicit in this irrational consumer behavior by encouraging these purchases or looking the other way if the math of affordability didn't seem to add up. Even the investment industry exacerbated the problems by miscalculating the risks of packaging these sub-prime loans together to create what they deemed high-quality, AAA-rated, mortgage-backed securities.

In reality, people act irrationally in their economic decisions. Driven by unforeseen motivations, we tend to make decisions that are not always in our best interest. We don't necessarily do this with bad intentions. Spending, saving, and managing a budget is hard, and we often try to find shortcuts to make it easier. Not only are we dealing with a wide range of outside influences and internal biases based on needs, wants, scarcity, financial stress, and mental capacity, but we also try to figure out most of it in our heads.

The complexities of "mental accounting" as well as the motivation behind our financial decisions has opened the doors for a whole new academic discipline called "behavioral economics" and it's gaining momentum as a mainstream course of study.

Connecting economics with psychology

The foundation for behavioral economics started in the 1970s with a pair of psychologists, Daniel Kahneman and Amos Tversky. They studied the cognitive biases that influence our behavior and their research showed that our decision-making did not line up with predicted economic models. Even though Kahneman's background and education was in psychology, he was awarded the 2002 Nobel Memorial Prize in Economic Sciences "for having integrated insights from psychological research into economic science, especially concerning human judgement and decision-making under uncertainty."

More recently, in October 2017, the Nobel Prize in the same category was awarded to Richard H. Thaler, professor of Behavioral Science and Economics at the University of Chicago's Booth School of Business. His award was for work in showing how people really behave—consistently defying economic theory.

As an aside, you may have seen Thaler in a cameo role in "The Big Short," the movie that chronicled the tragically-irrational housing market of the mid-2000s discussed earlier. In his scene, he sits at a blackjack table talking about one irrational behavior called the "hot hand fallacy," in which people think whatever is happening now will continue to happen into the future. The blackjack example is a metaphor for similar gambling behavior during the housing bubble: Let's make a BIG bet that housing prices will always go up. Not only that, we'll make even BIGGER side bets on it doing so. Then 2008 happened, and reality crashed the party.

Getting back to personal finance, Thaler's two most recent books, *Nudge: Improving Decisions About Health, Wealth and Happiness*[1] and, more recently, *Misbehaving: The Making of Behavioral Economics*[2], as well as Daniel Kahneman's book *Thinking Fast and Slow*[3], dive into how our minds operate in two very different systems of thought. One is an intuitive system, which is quick, emotional, and automatic, and the second is a rational system, which is slow, deliberate, and reflective.

Economics as a social science can help us *plan* rather than *do*

In *Misbehaving*, Thaler focuses on lack of self-control as a major obstacle to planning and thinking aimed at good, long-term decisions rather than taking the shortcut route that ignores any future impact. He introduces the name *Planner* for our more rational, long-term thinking self, and *Doer* for our impulsive, you-only-live-once nature. Today, the Planner in us might be able to take a reflective point of view and lay out a solid financial plan and budget, but as decision points come to us day-by-day, the Doer's impulsive behavior can ruin those well-intentioned plans.

Sound familiar? As he states in the book, "Most of us realize that we have self-control problems, but we underestimate their severity." To make progress toward a goal of financial freedom, you must work to improve your self-control.

At this point, some of you may be thinking, "Here we go. Sucking the fun out of life." We think of austerity and rules, then guilt when we break our rules. Is that where our lives need to go to overcome financial stress?

Actually, no, says Thaler. After decades of research, he knows better than anyone that people just won't buy into that.

To begin to find a better way, he ran an experiment around retirement savings. The first step was to find out why people were not saving enough. He identified three primary reasons:

- Inertia – Most of us know we should be saving more and plan to increase our savings. Then we procrastinate and make no changes.
- Loss aversion – Nobody wants less take-home pay.
- Future versus present self-control – Today we can look ahead and agree to increase retirement contributions; for example, every January 1. Then, come the new year, our present-bias says no again to reducing our take-home paycheck.

To overcome these issues, Thaler developed the "Save More Tomorrow" plan. Employees would agree to increase savings with every future pay raise. The retirement plan automated the increases so employees would avoid future decisions and never see a pay decrease. In four years, employees using the plan had quadrupled their savings rate from 3.5 percent to 13.6 percent.

On the other hand, those who didn't go with "Save More Tomorrow" but intended to increase savings on their own generally got stuck and made no further increases.

So there are ways we can help our inner Planner prevail and still find contentment. In fact, we'll share some techniques that can help you make progress and reward yourself at the same time a little later in this book. In the meantime, we can at least be aware of how our mind works when we engage in mental accounting.

More on the biases that affect our financial decisions

As Thaler has said: "In order to do good economics, you have to keep in mind that people are human." Being aware of your Planner-Doer battle allows you to be on the lookout for how your mind really works as you choose how to allocate and spend money.

Decision-making suffers when we let the automatic mind have its way, yet it is absolutely consistent with our human nature. We only have so much time to consider every purchase or financial decision, so our mind takes shortcuts when we make choices. These shortcuts, or *heuristics*, are our mind's way of reducing the amount of time and effort it takes to make decisions. These quick and easy heuristics help us by not allowing our minds to be overburdened by the daunting task of evaluating the options and outcomes of every decision, especially if they are similar to previous decisions we have made.

Whether you are choosing where to shop, what to eat at your favorite restaurant, or the products you buy and how much you are willing to pay, these heuristics influence you. While these shortcuts are intended to help you problem-solve, there are some unintended negative side effects. Much like the "tunneling" discussed in the previous chapter, which narrows our focus when dealing with scarcity, these heuristics can cause us to overlook or ignore information needed to make the best decision. They have the potential to do more harm than good.

Another good resource on this topic is the book *Dollars and Sense: How We Misthink Money and How to Spend Smarter,* by Dan Ariely and Jeff Kreisler.[4]

Ariely, a professor of psychology and behavioral economics at Duke University, has made a career of studying and writing about how irrational we are. He illustrates many mental shortcuts (or biases) in his book. Not all are included here, but the following sections provide you with an idea of how many different ways our minds manipulate our spending decisions. This information can help you understand your thinking when it comes to making changes to your spending habits.

Anchoring – how retailers use "regular price" to make you spend

We have a hard time assessing the true value of things, so we often look for clues or insight to point us in the right direction. We don't want to use too much mental effort to determine a fair price—that's too much work. Instead, we want to take a shortcut. We accept suggestions and base our decisions on them. Retailers take full advantage of this weakness in their pricing schemes. They are more than happy to offer "suggested retail" or "regular prices" before enticing you with discounts.

We have probably all heard the proverb that first impressions are the most lasting, or the famous Will Rogers quote: "You never get a second chance to make a first impression." Once retailers plant this "anchor" pricing impression in our minds, it's hard to disregard no matter how relevant it is to making a good decision.

In another Ariely book, *Predictably Irrational: The Hidden Forces That Shape Our Decisions*[5], he uses an experiment to show how irrational anchoring can be. He introduces a list of items:

a keyboard, computer mouse, a couple bottles of wine, a book, and some chocolates. Then he asks subjects to write down the last two digits of their Social Security number. To further associate these irrelevant and virtually random numbers, he asks the subjects to place a dollar sign in front of this two-digit number and select which of the items on the list they would pay this arbitrary amount for. As you can imagine, if your Social Security number ended in a low set of numbers you may be more willing to buy all the items at that price than if your Social Security number ended in a higher number.

The last request in this experiment was to ask subjects to list what each item was worth. The last two Social Security digits should have no bearing on what random items are worth or what people would be willing to pay, but in fact these random digits anchored a starting price. Those subjects with higher last-digit combinations were willing to pay much more for the items on the list.

Relativity – how you determine value relative to other things

Much like anchoring, we take otherwise irrelevant information and determine the relative value of things. If you were shopping for an item and discovered you could save $20 by driving five minutes to visit another store offering the same product for less, would you do it? It probably depends on the relationship of savings to the total cost for the item. If you were trying to buy something worth $40, then $20 would be a significant discount. But what if your potential purchase was $1,000? Would the $20 savings be worth the five-minute drive?

Even though in both cases a five-minute drive would equal $20, most people would not consider the savings to be worth it in the second example. Twenty dollars is $20 and a five-minute drive is a five-minute drive. If we were thinking rationally, the percentage savings represented by the $20 should not matter.

How would you gauge the value of something if you couldn't compare it to anything else? When Williams-Sonoma, a high-end specialty cookware retail store, introduced the first bread machine to the market for $275, it didn't sell very well. That price could have scared off potential buyers since it was about 275 times what it cost to simply buy a loaf of bread at the store. But the reality was that, since it was the first of its kind, consumers just didn't have anything with which to compare it and gauge its value.

To deal with this marketing flop, the retail store hired a marketing research firm to help them understand the sales slump. The solution was to introduce a second, slightly-better bread machine at a $400 price point, or about 50% higher than the cost of the original model. Relative to the more expensive model, the $275 option, which was almost as good, seemed more valuable. When consumers had the opportunity to compare the two options and determine the relative value between them, bread machines started flying off the shelf.

Descriptive language – features and benefits overload

When we compare different goods and services to determine value, we rely on information about our choices. The information we use to make decisions can sometimes be overwhelming. When we don't know how to analyze information, we become more trusting of outside opinions and are more open to suggestions. We form our opinions about quality, value, and price from the language used to describe our choices.

Think about the last time you bought a computer, TV, or other item with an extensive list of technical specs. The characteristics and attributes are listed in a way that sound impressive even if you have no idea what they mean. Do you want an 80-inch, 4K, ultra high definition, QLED liquid crystal display, curved-screen, smart TV with high dynamic range picture, 240hz motion rate, digital surround sound with audio depth enhancer, and a voice-controlled universal remote? I'm not only out of breath, but I'm confused too.

If you don't know what all those features mean, how would you determine what this TV is worth? In this case, we're apt to assign value based on comparing the descriptions of two products. There is no need to know what a feature is and what it does to compare it to another product.

If you were to compare our full-featured TV to other TVs, you would probably see a pricing scheme that lines up size and features with price in a linear way. Smaller TVs with fewer features would equal lower prices, and larger TVs with more features would equal higher prices. Even if you have no idea what these features mean, you would probably consider the TV with the most features at the lowest price, relative to the other TVs, to be the best bang for your buck.

Language and imagery also have the power to influence our feelings about the products we are evaluating and even our willingness to buy. Compare the menu of a fancy farm-to-table restaurant with a more budget-friendly chain restaurant. The descriptions on the menu at the upscale venue explain the intricate details of flavors, ingredients, and how they are prepared. Unless you know the skill necessary to acquire, assemble, and prepare the ingredients into the magnificent meal being described, can you really use that information to determine the value?

Now look at the wine menu. What year, varietal, and region should you consider when pairing a good wine with your meal? Perhaps a sophisticated connoisseur with a discerning palate can analyze the options and make a good choice, but if that's not you, would you be open to suggestion? If that recommendation is coming from a master sommelier then you can probably expect to pay a lot of money. If, on the other hand, you are left to choose your pairing, you might be tempted to just pick based on price, figuring that more expensive wine will be better.

Overemphasizing money – higher price must mean better value

When we can't evaluate something, we also associate higher prices with more value. Like our examples of a high-tech smart TV, or the detail-rich restaurant menu and wine list, quality and price are correlated. We assume that an item with a higher price must be better than an item with a lower price. This idea is reinforced every time you buy a lower-cost product that does not live up to your expectations, or the high expectations you have of the higher-cost alternative. We almost feel as though we deserve to have the cheap substitute fail because "you get what you pay for." This is not exactly a rational thought if you based your decision on the features and specifications of what you need, rather than the cost relative to other comparable products.

When you put this kind of thinking together with the language and pricing schemes marketers use, along with our tendency to anchor and use relativity in making our purchasing decisions, you can see that we are at a clear disadvantage.

Certainly, influence directed from the outside affects our decision making, but what about the things we do to fool ourselves? The following introduces some of our own irrational decision-making behaviors.

Illusory superiority – the above-average effect

Curiosity didn't kill the cat, it was likely overconfidence. People tend to believe that they can do more than they are capable of. This doesn't mean that we suffer from delusions of greatness or believe we have superhuman capabilities. We make assumptions about what other average people can do and believe that we are probably just as good—if not a little better—than they are.

Much like the perception that most drivers believe they are better than average, which we discussed in the first chapter, people tend to believe they are better than they really are at everyday tasks. When it comes to mental accounting, we tend to have an unrealistic overconfidence that we can do a lot of math in our heads.

Availability – miscalculating risk and reward

In addition to our overconfidence in performing everyday tasks, we also tend to believe that rare or infrequent events happen more frequently than they really do. Quickly determining the likelihood of an event can help us decide if the risk is worth the benefit. We can get into trouble if we combine our overconfidence with miscalculated odds of success.

When you hear about a car accident, especially one resulting in serious injury or death, it makes an impression in your mind. The significance of that event causes you to remember it. Even though the actual odds of being involved in a fatal crash are relatively small, you are more aware of the consequence and believe it to be more likely than it really is.

Something much less significant than a car accident but still memorable is the number of times you come to a red light on your daily commute. You must slow down, come to a stop and wait before you can proceed, which, if you are in a hurry, is much more memorable than passing through a green light. By the time you make it home after a long day of work, it's easy to believe you hit every red light!

On a more positive note, examples of picking the next hot investment or winning the lottery stand out in your mind as more memorable than someone who did not make their fortune overnight. You may recognize that the odds are slim, but exactly how slim is a common miscalculation, which could lead you to believe that the relationship between risk and reward is much more in your favor than in reality.

Affect – trusting your gut feelings

Much like the availability heuristic, the *affect heuristic* allows us to quickly assess risks and benefits. This heuristic, however, relies on our feelings when quickly making decisions, rather than using analysis of facts or real possibilities and outcomes. This emotional evaluation of pros and cons is based on the positive or negative feelings generated by a situation or result—a gut reaction.

If the feeling of risk or cost is greater than the benefit, then you would likely conclude that it's not worth it. If, on the other hand, the positive feelings associated with the benefits are greater than the negative feelings associated with the consequences, you will likely decide to go after the benefit.

While this heuristic can help you to make decisions quickly without the need to process and evaluate information, you can easily be deceived. The more directly an outcome can be attributed to the cause, the more accurate your emotional responses will be. However, if you don't immediately recognize negative outcomes, there is a chance they will never be included in your emotional reaction.

If you feel stress over your finances, it is likely the result of many poor financial decisions and not easily attributable to one specific expense or purchase. Yet you can easily recall the positive feelings associated with individual purchases. Your gut feelings about spending can be skewed toward the positive benefits of immediate gratification rather than the stress of living beyond your means.

Confirmation bias – reconfirming past decisions…right or wrong

We base future decisions on past decisions. Not only is this a shortcut that saves time and effort in rethinking past purchases, but it serves as validation that our previous decision was a good one. If you paid a certain price for a particular brand in the past, it is easy to simply accept that as the status quo and never rethink whether a different brand at a better price would offer more value.

We intentionally seek information that reaffirms our bias. Even when presented with evidence that we may have been wrong, we selectively ignore that information to avoid admitting our error and putting more thought toward solving the problem again.

Understanding these biases does not prevent you from falling for them. Even if you recognize the cognitive biases affecting others, the better-than-average effect can kick in, creating a *bias blind spot* that allows you to think you are not nearly as affected as the average person.

Herding – going with the crowd

Much like the desire to validate our past decisions with confirmation bias, we tend to look to others for help making decisions. When we trust that other people have evaluated all the options and come to the best conclusion, we save the time and effort of deciding for ourselves. This willingness to go with the crowd comes from our assumption that something must be good if a lot of other people are doing it. A long wait for a table at a popular restaurant or a line outside a store to get the latest product release reinforces the appeal.

Herding also stems from a survival instinct. We experience the benefit of safety and protection when we are part of a group as opposed to being by ourselves. This sense of safety makes us more willing to follow along with others. These groups can serve to endorse products, styles, and fashion trends that influence our behavior. Our desire to fit in with these groups can cause us to conform our tastes, preferences, and beliefs to what the group finds good or bad, rather than making our best decision.

Overvalue expectations – expectations change our experience

Information about a product or service can distort our judgment of the true value or our preference. Most interesting is that, when we have higher expectations for a product, it changes our actual experience and enjoyment. MRIs of subjects during experiments on this topic show that our brains activate to make the experience live up to our expectation.

In a paper titled "Try It, You'll Like It: The Influence of Expectation, Consumption, and Revelation on Preferences for Beer,"[6] Dan Ariely and his colleagues arrived at this conclusion by offering beer taste tests using a "secret ingredient."

That ingredient was balsamic vinegar. Most of us would think right away, "That sounds disgusting." For the experiment, one group of tasters was not told about the vinegar, one group was told before they tasted, and the third was told after they had consumed the beer.

Actual results showed that those not told of the added vinegar liked the beer much more. On the other hand, those told following the taste had only slightly less preference. Finally, those told before they tasted experienced the expectations phenomenon at work. The majority of this final group, anticipating a bad experience, did not like the beer with vinegar at all. They expected the experience to be disgusting, and it was. It was not because of the actual taste, but because they activated their brains and senses to fulfill their expectation.

Ariely said the results show how we color our perceptions as we make choices in two ways:

- Bottom-up process – actual use of product and how our senses are stimulated by the experience.
- Top-down process – our beliefs, desires, and expectations, which set us up to get the experience we want.

The paper includes a list of studies that have confirmed the same distortion of true value by our minds:

- Coke was rated higher when consumed from a cup with the Coke logo.
- A slice of turkey rated higher among subjects when they were told it was a popular brand, compared to an unpopular one.
- Perrier water was preferred to generic seltzer water if it carried the Perrier label, but not otherwise.
- Bitter coffee was perceived as less so when subjects were repeatedly misinformed that it was not bitter.

The result is that our experience of a product is a mixture of reality and what we expect. If we're convinced that we need to buy only brand name products because they are "better," generic or store brands will taste worse to us. Unless we fight the urge to overvalue expectations, we'll probably overspend when it comes to meeting these needs. The high-end TV will look and sound better, we'll prefer the $15 restaurant burger over the $5 fast-food version, and the most expensive wine will surely beat anything costing less.

Endowment effect – one man's trash is probably not another man's treasure

Our expectations are not the only bias that affect how we perceive value. Ownership can also determine how valuable we believe something to be. In most cases, the owner of an item will value it higher simply because they own it.

In "Anomalies: The Endowment Effect, Loss Aversion, and Status Quo Bias,"[7] a study by Daniel Kahneman, Richard Thaler, and Jack Knetsch, coffee mugs were handed out to a group of students. The students were then asked what they would accept as payment if someone wanted to buy the mug from them. A second group of students was then asked how much they would be willing to pay for the same mug. The students who were asked if they would like to buy the mug averaged a value of $3, while student who owned the mugs valued them at an average of $7.

When you have ownership of something, you take into consideration the usefulness of the item, the memories, and the hard work you have put into caring for and maintaining it. It has an intrinsic value that only you can see.

When others look at it, they see only what it is *relative* to other things. They are not biased by the same things that make you believe it's worth more.

Now in the case of a coffee mug, you might not see the emotional attachment. Instead, take a house or a car as an example. You have an emotional attachment to it because it has provided significant utility to you and your daily life. You remember the effort and the money put into customizing, maintaining or restoring it. Most people come to believe that the value of that home or car includes the effort, gratitude, and love they have poured into the item.

How does this bias impact our financial decisions and well-being?

It's probably the reason why someone will spend $1,000 a year to store $500 worth of stuff in a storage unit—or not want to downsize to a smaller home. (What will you do with all your stuff?)

This effect can also play into sales and marketing efforts to influence consumption. Examples include free samples, trial memberships, test driving a vehicle, or trying on makeup at the department store cosmetics counter. Marketers use these "try it before you buy it" techniques to stimulate a sense of ownership and leverage the endowment effect to get you closer to purchasing.

Whether it's a "100% money-back satisfaction guarantee" or a "buy now, pay later" offer, these are ways to get you to take ownership without the risk of buyer's remorse. Once it's in your possession and you feel like it's worth what you paid, you won't want to give it back.

Hyperbolic discounting – immediate-self discounts future-self

We tend to overemphasize the value of something right now and discount the value of something in the future. As an example, imagine you were offered $100 right now or $110 in a week. If you are like most, you would likely take the $100 today even though waiting a week would yield a 10 percent increase. We do this because we naturally separate our future-self from our current-self and discount the value that our future-self would receive compared to what our current-self can have.

Consider the same example with a slight change. What if you were offered $100 in one year or $110 in one year and one week? Most likely you'll wait the extra week to get the extra 10 percent increase. In this case, the money is not immediately available for you either way, it's only available for future you, so your brain doesn't engage in this discounting.

Filing for Social Security is another perfect example of how hyperbolic discounting affects our decision-making. You have three choices for drawing Social Security: As early as 62, at your full retirement age, or delayed until age 70.

At age 62, you can take the income at a discount to what you would receive in the future, and according to the Center for Retirement Research at Boston College, a clear majority of people do just that. In a 2015 study titled "Trends in Social Security Claiming,"[8] only 10 percent waited until after their full retirement age to draw Social Security, with 56 percent of men and 64 percent of women choosing to draw Social Security before turning 65.

Compartmentalizing – the urge to splurge with "extra" money

We compartmentalize our money when we assign different value to it based on its source. Think about how you might spend a bonus or tax refund differently from regular wages. We like to relax our spending discipline and splurge on a "reward" for ourselves when we get what we perceive as extra money.

It's not rational to treat money differently because of how we get it, but it seems sensible because we're not violating a budget—this "extra" money was never a part of it. The consequence of losing it seems less painful because we would be in the same place whether we had the money or not.

Imagine a scenario in which you're gambling in a casino. You're willing to risk $20 for the chance of winning and you feed a crisp $20 bill into a slot machine. You pull the handle and win $200! All the excitement of the win along with loud chimes, bright flashing lights, and $200 to play again encourages you to keep on gambling. After some losses, your $200 turns into $180. Would you stop gambling? You started off willing to spend $20, but because your mind naturally compartmentalizes your original $20 from the additional winnings, it is highly likely that you don't consider loss of winnings to be the same as loss of "your" money.

If you stopped gambling and walked away with your winnings, how would you describe your gambling experience? Did you win $160, or did you lose $20? Most would answer that they won. You started with $20 and walked away with $180. Pretty easy math to determine that you're now $160 richer. But at one point you had $200, and now you have only $180. You lost $20.

Compartmentalizing also pertains to spending. Whether you have formally budgeted for housing, utilities and other ongoing expenses, or you are relying on mental accounting, you assign different values to these categories based on the priority you place on fulfilling them.

Out with friends for a night of dinner and entertainment, spending $200 on overpriced food and drinks can be easily accepted and enjoyed. Spending $200 on something much less enjoyable like your electric bill, and depending on how you prioritize these categories, might feel much more painful.

Avoiding pain – separating consumption from the "pain" of spending

It should come as no surprise that you would rather not experience pain, or that you will go to great lengths to avoid it. The mere fact that you are alive today is probably in some way a testimony to this concept. Pain has allowed you to learn through experience what is dangerous, and to not do those things again. Like a child touching a hot stove, some things you only do once.

But as sophisticated as our nervous system is, it is just an indicator helping us to recognize pain. We have plenty of ways to still do what we want and either avoid the pain or protect ourselves from it.

Sometimes we can clearly see the potential for pain. The speed of a hockey puck off a professional slap shot can easily reach 100 mph. The size and weight of the puck along with that kind of velocity can do quite a bit of damage to what or who gets in its way. The potential for pain does not stop some people from playing hockey or blocking that shot. It does, however, warrant the use of protective gear to prevent some of the pain associated with it.

Our decision to expose ourselves to potential pain can be managed by either our ability to avoid it (protect ourselves) or deal with it (take medication). But how would our decisions differ if the consequence of pain was not immediately connected with its cause?

Consider the aftermath of spending too much time in the sun without sunscreen. In the moment of outdoor recreation, everything may seem fine. You may not be immediately aware of the developing sunburn or the pain that will result. Your ability to make a good decision, like putting on sunscreen, may be affected by your inability to recognize the coming pain.

Now let's take this one step further. What if you had the ability to intentionally delay the feeling of pain associated with any activity? In the moment, you would have the best of both worlds. You get what you want, without any perceivable pain, similar to taking a painkiller to numb its effects. This is where some of our decisions around dealing with pain parallel our financial lives.

The feeling of spending money can be painful. It may not be as physically painful as being hit with a speeding hockey puck, but there is discomfort. You worked hard to earn your money and parting with it can be a reminder of all that effort. The pain of paying diminishes the pleasure of buying.

The painkiller of choice in this case is credit cards or debt financing. It separates the joy of consumption from the pain of parting with our hard-earned cash. Of course, the decision to put off payment until a later time is unsustainable if it extends you beyond your means. Just like that sunburn, in due time you'll feel the pain.

Overcoming our irrational tendencies

We need to be aware of the ways we talk ourselves into spending money. We don't rationally line up the pros and cons, then make the proper call. In general, we don't have enough time or information to do that for most purchases. And even if we did, we're unaware of the mental processes subconsciously skewing our purchase decisions.

This is the way our brains work. Even Ariely admits he doesn't have a cure. But there is one mental game he suggests to combat these urges. Ariely says we can "reconnect to our future-selves."

Here is an exercise you can use to pause and think about the dollars you are spending in the moment versus how those dollars might serve you better in the future. When you are considering spending money, think about the satisfaction that your immediate-self will experience, then imagine yourself looking back at this purchase from the future. Does your future-self share this same satisfaction? Will your future-self feel the pain of this purchase or suffer a consequence as a result of fulfilling this immediate desire? Perhaps there is an alternate use for this money that would satisfy both your immediate-self and your future-self.

Ariely says the technique works best when you've set specific goals, with dollar amounts and a timeline. Then you have a real framework to use this "back to the future" exercise to make better purchase judgements through the years.

Ariely is on the money (pardon the pun) with that, and we'll describe how to set measurable goals in Chapter 6.

Now that we understand a little bit about how the human mind affects the way we spend to fulfill our needs, let's explore our individual motivations to spend.

Chapter Notes

1) *Nudge: Improving Decisions About Health, Wealth and Happiness*, Richard Thaler, Penguin Books, 2008

2) *Misbehaving: The Making of Behavioral Economics*, Richard Thaler, W.W. Norton & Company, 2015

3) *Thinking Fast and Slow*, Daniel Kahneman, Farrar, Straus & Giroux, 2011

4) *Dollars and Sense: How We Misthink Money and How to Spend Smarter,* Dan Ariely and Jeff Kreisler, Harper Collins Publishers, 2017

5) *Predictably Irrational: The Hidden Forces That Shape Our Decisions*, Dan Ariely, Harper Perennial, 2008

6) "Try It, You'll Like It: The Influence of Expectation, Consumption, and Revelation on Preferences for Beer;" Leonard Lee, Shane Frederick, and Dan Ariely; *Association for Psychological Science*, Vol. 17, No. 12

7) "Anomalies: The Endowment Effect, Loss Aversion, and Status Quo Bias;" Daniel Kahneman, Richard Thaler, and Jack Knetsch, *Journal of Economic Perspectives*, Vol. 5, No. 1, Winter 1991, American Economic Association

8) "Trends in Social Security Claiming," Center for Retirement Research at Boston College, Number 15-8, May 2015

4: Exploring Our Motivations to Spend

"Wax on, wax off."
— *Mr. Miyagi ("The Karate Kid," Columbia Pictures, 1984)*

The phrase "wax on, wax off" was an iconic theme from the movie "The Karate Kid." A young boy named Daniel was expecting to learn karate from his teacher Mr. Miyagi. Instead, he was subjected to what he thought were meaningless chores. One was waxing cars for Mr. Miyagi.

The teacher wanted this task done in a very specific way: Wax on with the right hand, circling clockwise, wax off with the left hand, circling counterclockwise. Miyagi also told him to breathe in through his nose and out through his mouth as he worked.

Daniel didn't understand the purpose of the work at first. But over time, he learned that the "wax on, wax off" movements made it easier to learn karate techniques. Just like Daniel, we also need to understand that learning new skills or changing behaviors is not a matter of just "doing it," but takes time and patience.

Remember our Chapter 1 reference to the screenplay plotline as a parallel to the pursuit of financial freedom? We are in the second stage, gaining awareness of a "new situation," working our way toward Turning Point 2 and a "change of plans."

In the same way that Daniel needed to learn the basic movements to be proficient in karate, we need to understand the psychological motivations that drive us and the irrational ways we make decisions so that we may better understand why we spend money the way we do.

Why do we want the things we buy? Are they truly necessary? Where is our desire to spend coming from? Are we aware of the big-picture implications of our consumption? Are we leading our financial future or falling prey to someone else's plan?

Knowing the answers to these questions will help us prioritize and compromise on our spending so that we can fulfill our needs while staying within our means. We can find contentment in a new lifestyle, while building the discretionary margin we want and finding a balance between what we make and what we spend. By separating our wants from our true needs, we can reduce our overall financial burden, reduce stress, and provide a greater sense of financial freedom.

Price vs value

Living within your means requires that you not only identify and separate your needs from your wants, but also determine how much you are going to spend to satisfy either of those categories. We have to weigh the price we pay along with the value of what we are consuming. Those terms may seem interchangeable, but it is important to see the difference.

The value of anything is derived from its usefulness, quality, features, and benefits. Value is a measure of how important something is to *you*. Price on the other hand is merely a representation of value based on what *others* are either willing to pay or accept in exchange. Price is a function of the economic principal of supply and demand and is affected by forces outside of your control. How abundant or scarce something is or how badly people want it should have little bearing on how valuable something is to you. However, it absolutely affects the price you pay.

Everything is ultimately worth what people are willing to pay and when you want something so badly that you mistakenly consider it to be a need, then you become more willing to pay a price that is justified by an artificial value. When you combine this with the heuristics and cognitive biases that affect our spending decisions, you can see that we need to clearly identify if we are either: 1) being influenced to want something so badly that we believe we *need* it, or 2) being influenced to pay an unwarranted price.

Acting in our own best interest

Whether it is influence from peers or marketers, we end up being encouraged to consume right up to the limit of our available resources. Our mental accounting keeps track of what we believe those resources are, exposing us to some poor judgments about our spending.

We learned about confirmation bias and how we go to great lengths to avoid admitting we were wrong about previous decisions. That bias applies to the decisions we've made about what we consider to be our needs and/or our wants.

We also learned about hedonic adaptation and our ability to grow accustomed to our lifestyles at every income level as well as hyperbolic discounting and the difficulty we face when deciding between immediate desires and future benefits. If our income increases, we quickly adjust our lifestyle expenses to meet our available resources and, thanks to confirmation bias, those spending decisions can be hard to unwind.

There are many heuristics and cognitive biases that either allow us to deceive ourselves or make us more susceptible to being deceived by others. When you put all this together you begin to see some of the challenges that these mental shortcuts present in our ability to act in our own best interest both today and into the future.

Measuring up to the greatest hits

Social media has led us down a road that encourages more consumption at an unsustainable level as we try to keep up with others. Facebook, Instagram, Pinterest, and other social channels present us with a world that is visually connected as never before. Even though we may not be close personal friends, we see more and more of how others are living—or how we *think* they are living. As with the herding heuristic or the psychological needs we discussed in Chapter 2, it's human nature to want to fit in. Our desires for social belonging or to meet our esteem needs create pressure to own more stuff, experience more, or live a certain lifestyle.

What we often overlook is that social media shows us everyone's "greatest hits" album. We tend to always compare their fun times and highlights with our overall life.

They've summed up an entire day with three or four pictures of a great meal or an amazing experience. They posted an album of photos from a week on vacation, their new car, or their perfectly staged selfie in some exciting place. What we don't see is a picture of the bill or the credit card statement. We see only the best of what they have or what they are doing, and we think we should be able to do it too.

More than likely, you're trying to keep up with something that's not even real. Would it surprise you to learn that in 2017 the average American household was carrying $15,000 in credit card debt?[1] Do you think your Facebook friends or the couple next door are the exceptions?

The result is that we tend to inflate who we are, then compare ourselves to someone who has likely inflated who they are—all of us asking, "Am I accepted and doing a good enough job to keep up with others?" The urge to keep up with the Joneses is certainly a powerful motivator, and this way of thinking can easily lead us into temptations to spend. You must make sure you know what you are really trying to keep up with.

Ignoring opportunity cost

As discussed with hyperbolic discounting, we have a hard time recognizing the future value of something when the alternative involves an immediate benefit. It begs the question, are we unaware of the future value or do we simply choose to ignore it? If you know that something is wrong and you do it anyway, then you probably deserve the consequence. We like to believe that the opposite is true if we end up making a mistake and didn't know it was wrong. Either way we're stuck with the consequences, deserving or not.

It's not always easy to understand your options, but making good decisions requires you to at least know your choices. You may be familiar with the Robert Frost poem "The Road Not Taken." In it, he describes a scene in which he made a choice between two paths that diverged in the woods, recognizing that each path offered different opportunities. He finished the poem by observing that his choice for taking the path less traveled has made all the difference. As Frost reflected on his choice, he could identify what choosing the other path might have meant for his life.

When we make spending decisions our choices are not always as clearly defined as two distinct paths. The idea of opportunity cost goes beyond simply looking at our decision to either spend or not spend money. Unlike Frost's poem, which looks back to choices already made, opportunity cost in spending decisions should be about recognizing all the other options for your dollars at the moment of choice, including your financial goals or other future purchases. Those opportunities are lost with each dollar that you spend.

It's one thing to look at small purchases of $5 here or $10 there and consider other ways you could have used that money. Or to add up what all those little expenses would amount to if they were never spent. A much more powerful calculation is what those little amounts could be worth 30, 40, or 50 years into the future.

A quote from Warren Buffett, one of the most successful investors and money managers of all time, in the Alice Schroeder biography *The Snowball*, illustrates this point: "Do I really want to spend $300,000 for this haircut?"

As ridiculous as that price may seem, Buffett didn't just look at the amount saved. He assumed an alternative use for that money, which could grow over many decades to be worth a much larger amount. Confidence in his ability to achieve exceptional investment returns allowed him to consider significant opportunity cost of even the most insignificant expenses.

The value of money over time goes beyond just increasing by a set percentage. It is an exponential increase from compound growth, as the interest from the original balance then gains interest on the interest. This snowballing effect just needs a lot of time and patience to pay off. This is where opportunity costs can really add up.

The rule of 72

Since we use mental accounting for so many of our spending decisions, the "rule of 72" is an easy way to calculate compound interest in your head. If you divide 72 by an annual rate of return, the result will be the number of years it will take for an amount to double in value at that rate of return. Here's an example:

A 5% annual rate of return would double your balance in 14.4 years (72 ÷ 5 = 14.4)

The question now becomes, what is a good rate of return to assume? I could go into a long, well-thought-out argument about long-term economic growth, inflation, capital market averages, and dividend rates and make the case that 7% to 8% would be a reasonable number. But we want to simplify the math, right? So let's use 7.2% because it divides into 72 so easily. That leaves us with an easy-to-calculate formula for quickly assessing future value when considering opportunity cost. Your money would double every 10 years.

For every $100 you spent in your 20s, it would have been worth $200 in your 30s, $400 in your 40s, $800 in your 50s, $1,600 in your 60s, $3,200 in your 70s, $6,400 in your 80s, and $12,800 in your 90s.

What the heck were you doing in your 20s with that money that was so important? Can you remember a fraction of the things you spent your money on back then? For that matter, what are you consuming today and why? Does it fulfill your needs and have a positive impact on your life or is some of it wasted on things you don't need, want, or even like?

If it comes down to doing some quick math in the checkout line to reconsider your purchase, what other last-minute considerations can save you from spending money on something you don't need?

Minimalism

Consider the lifestyle transformations of minimalists Joshua Fields Millburn and Ryan Nicodemus, authors of *Everything That Remains: A Memoir by the Minimalists*, and founders of theminimalists.com. They both left successful, high-paying careers in search of a life with more meaning than what their paychecks could provide.

They recognized that the stuff they owned represented a burden they had to carry with them in their day-to-day lives.

If you were to backpack into a remote location for a weeklong camping trip, you might put some consideration into the things you take with you. You would likely evaluate the purpose of every item you place in your backpack to maximize efficiency while minimizing the load or weight you had to carry.

Your home is basically your backpack. In addition to living in that space, you're storing all the stuff essential to your life. Millburn and Nicodemus have tapped into a higher level of happiness by lightening their loads. They have placed a priority on the things that have purpose and meaning, letting go of anything that does not make the cut.

If you feel a need to declutter and reduce the burden of carrying around all your stuff, I encourage you to read more from "The Minimalists." But you can also use this same mindset when presented with the opportunity to spend money. Will this thing or experience provide you joy? Have significant meaning to you? Have purpose or add value to your life?

If your backpack can only hold so much, would you be willing to give up something else in your life to make room for this new purchase?

Impacts of consumption

Spending and consuming are pleasurable activities and making changes to consume less can seem limiting or leave you feeling deprived. But consumption is about more than just using up your personal resources. What's the ultimate impact? If the net result is positive for you and your family—or the world—that's a win.

While this book is not about telling you how you should or shouldn't spend your money, there is a growing consciousness concerning the global impacts of what we consume. If environmental issues are important to you and your family, then why would you not factor that into your consumption decisions? It may be a last-minute objection that encourages you to rethink your spending decision.

Take a look at some of these facts (and a few ways to make positive impacts with your decisions). Changing your spending habits may not only come easier, but be emotionally rewarding as well:

- **Plastics**: About 30 million tons of plastic are discarded every year, with only about 10 percent recycled. Every year about 8 million metric tons of that plastic makes its way into the ocean.[2] To look at this by volume, that's a fleet of over 700 aircraft carriers worth of plastic setting sail every year!*

  (Buy fewer single-use beverage bottles, choose items with less packaging, consider buying pre-owned children's toys or other items that have a short timeline for use.)

- **E-waste**: With rapid technology change, electronic waste has become a significant contributor to our landfills. According to earth911.com, Americans throw away 9.4 million tons of e-waste every year. A Gallup[3] poll found that only 54% of smartphone users say they wait until their phone is not functional or obsolete before replacing it. Some plastic, heavy metals, and chemicals can be reclaimed, but the hydrochloric acid used in the process can create worse problems than just discarding it.

  (Replace consumer electronics only when necessary, rather than always buying the newer, faster, better upgrade.)

---

*Math based on approximate 88,000 metric ton displacement of a fully loaded Nimitz class aircraft carrier. https://www.public.navy.mil/airfor/cvn71pages/factsandfigures.aspx
Volume calculated on approximate difference in density between metal and plastic of 7.8 times.

- **Carbon Footprint**: For every gallon of gasoline saved as a result of more efficient vehicle miles-per-gallon performance, approximately 24 pounds of carbon emissions are avoided. Greenhouse gas and oil pollution from air and sea shipping is also growing every year.
  (Rethink purchases from online retailers or other goods delivered by container ships and airfreight from around the world. Choose smaller, more efficient vehicles and reduce vehicle trips to cut direct pollution, conserve resources, and reduce additional impacts from petroleum exploration, transportation, and distribution.)

- **Food Waste**: Per capita food waste is over 660 pounds annually in North America, according to the United Nations. Americans throw away $165 billion in food per year. That's $2,200 per average household.[4] It's more than just throwing away money. The resources used to grow it, process it, deliver it, and prepare it come with a cost as well.
  (Buy less perishable food in bulk, reduce restaurant trips, cook and serve smaller portions.)

The point of this book is not to convince people to become minimalists or to shame people into consuming less. You don't need to feel guilty about your past spending decisions or regret where your resources have gone. That won't get your money back. It's about being empowered in the moment to make decisions that line up with your beliefs and goals, right now and in the future. Think about *prioritizing* how you spend your money, rather than "cutting back."

Convenience

You may also notice a theme to some of our wasteful and unnecessary consumption: We are suckers for convenience. Whether it is the use of "disposable" plastic utensils or buying a new washer and dryer instead of fixing the old one, the convenience of our consumption guides our decisions. Think of all the things you've unnecessarily spent money on simply because it was convenient.

Convenience exposes an interesting pattern in our spending behavior. We take the path of least resistance. Retailers, especially online retailers, have focused on not just marketing their products but also making them easy to buy. That is the underlying motivation behind the "one click" option on Amazon or any website that wants to save your credit card information to make purchasing simple and easy. Encouraging you to buy has as much to do with ease of transaction as it does with the features and benefits of the product itself.

The paycheck-to-paycheck mentality

Do you spend money according to a plan or do you just consume indiscriminately based on whether you have access to money or not? Does your behavior or consumption change if it's payday or during the last few days leading up to payday?

A 2017 survey by CareerBuilder found that 78% of American workers lived paycheck to paycheck.[5] Whether you think of yourself as living that way or not, it's a sure sign of this mentality when your willingness to spend is based on what's in your bank account, rather than what your budget dictates. The days immediately after payday may be filled with fun, while the days leading up to the next payday are not. Paydays are regular and consistent, but your spending is not.

Think about it in terms of your vehicle's gas tank. With a full tank we rarely think about how far we're going or whether we really need to make the trip. But with the gauge moving toward empty, we're suddenly aware of where we're going, how many miles it is, and when we can refuel. That last gallon of gas was always in the tank. What makes us suddenly more careful with that resource? We should be thinking about each gallon more carefully whether it's one of many or the last one.

Thinking about our bank account the same way will help us be smarter about our spending. Every dollar or one hundred dollars is a resource we need to use wisely, not burn until we hit empty.

Living paycheck to paycheck leaves you open to manipulation, both by external influences and your own "mental accounting" justifications, that unravels long-term financial planning. Maybe the worst downside to this lifestyle is that it leads to an overreliance on credit. You'll think "I'm good for it" because the money is coming. It's the mistake of thinking about what you have access to, as opposed to what you have. Credit cards can then become our own payday loan store, and a cycle of debt begins.

Learning about our motivations and spending patterns gives us the fundamentals we need to avoid deceiving ourselves. Ignoring opportunity costs, the time value of money, and the impacts of our consumption can keep us from our true goals. We touched briefly on it in this chapter, but now we'll dive deeper into how debt wastes our money and derails our plans.

Chapter Notes

1) "2017 American Household Credit Card Debt Survey," NerdWallet, https://www.nerdwallet.com/blog/credit-card-data

2) "Facts About Plastic," Plastic Oceans, https://plasticoceans.org/the-facts/

3) Gallup Panel, 2015, https://news.gallup.com/poll/184043/americans-split-often-upgrade-smartphones.aspx

4) "Food Matters: Food Waste," National Resource Defense Council, 2016, https://www.nrdc.org/stories/food-matters-food-waste

5) Career Builder Survey, 2017, http://press.careerbuilder.com2017-08-24-Living-Paycheck-to-Paycheck-is-a-Way-of-Life-for-Majority-of-U-S-Workers-According-to-New-CareerBuilder-Survey

5: Spending Money We Don't Have

"Americanism: Using money you haven't earned to buy things you don't need to impress people you don't like."
——*Robert Quillen, American journalist and humorist*

Dave Ramsey is often credited with a similar quote, but it was Quillen who first put the thought into words in the early 1900s. Regardless of the source, the truth behind it can't be disputed.

Marketers are motivated to sell you things and the first objection they have to overcome is getting you to spend money you don't have. Once they've convinced you to buy, they need to *enable* you to buy as well. Without credit, they can convince you, but signing the final deal might not happen. That's why car dealers or durable goods retailers like furniture and appliance stores enable you to apply right on the spot: "Do you want it? We'll figure out how you can have it."

It seems as though every big box retailer or department store offers some sort of immediate discount if you apply for their in-house credit card. Regardless of how much the final bill is, they make it a point to ask you to sign up. It doesn't matter if you turn them down this go-around, they have planted the seed for future purchases when you can not only get the discount, but you can also avoid the pain of having to part with your hard-earned money.

How many commercials have you seen that put more emphasis on the financing terms than the products they are marketing? Phrases like "zero money down" or "no payments until next year" entice us into satisfying our desire whether we have the money or not.

How about this offer from a rent-to-own furniture company? "Seven days and only $7 to be seven times happier!" That's it—They've figured out the magic formula for you to be happy! At least until you find out how many times you must pay that $7.

Or maybe this holiday appeal for a luxury vehicle: "Let out your inner child. Experience amazing!" Followed up, of course, with financing or lease terms that make it very easy to step up to a luxury car. That's right, throw out your adult reasoning and be like a kid, "I want it, and I'm getting it." "Amazing" for sure.

Do those sound like messages from people with your best interests in mind? Sounds more like lots of money behind lots of high-priced marketing folks thinking up ways to lure you in.

Meanwhile, the number of people delinquent on loans has been rising since 2011, even when unemployment was at its lowest point since 2000. Take auto loans, for example. In 2017, there were 6.3 million people at least 90 days behind on payments, according to the New York Federal Reserve. That was a six percent increase over 2016. And the average auto loan is $30,000. Yikes!

Ask yourself, "Am I being influenced or pushed to buy something that I otherwise couldn't?" If the credit terms, payment periods, or introductory offers are allowing you to make that choice, that's the red flag.

Price vs Actual Cost

Unless you live in a state with no sales tax, you're probably used to paying a different price at the cash register than what's on the price tag. Even if you do benefit from not having to pay sales tax you can probably relate to a bill with additional fees and charges added to the original, advertised cost.

Not all those extra charges are hidden. Some are completely up to you, like a gratuity for a job well done. All these differences between advertised price and actual cost are typically on the receipt so you still know exactly what you had to pay for the product or service consumed. What about premiums and discounts that are not so obvious?

There are three ways to pay for the things we consume:

- Save up for purchases and effectively pay in advance.
- Use available cash flow and pay in the moment.
- Borrow money and pay after the fact.

Depending on the way we make purchases and the timing of when money changes hands, the things we consume can have a different actual cost than what was on the price tag. This true cost can either be less than, equal to, or more than the listed price.

When you save toward the goal of a future purchase or expense there's a good chance you could collect interest on the money you set aside. Because of any growth or interest you receive, the amount you actually set aside could end up being less than the amount needed to make the purchase. This is much more evident over longer periods of time or with more costly items, but there are some other benefits that come with this approach.

The patience required to "save up" for an item may give you the time necessary to wait for a promotional discount or sale price. Because of typical product life cycles, you may simply see the price come down over the time you are saving toward your purchase. Or, you may just find that avoiding spontaneous purchases and taking time to carefully consider what you are buying allows you to re-think your decisions and prevents you from unnecessarily spending altogether.

Using available cash to pay for things in the moment, you pay the exact amount needed for the purchase. There is no specific advantage or disadvantage to this method. The actual cost and the list price are equal.

Borrowing money and paying after the fact will add cost beyond the price you paid at the point of sale. The interest rate and time it takes to pay off a loan can *dramatically* increase the total amount paid. Because amortization calculations can make it difficult to know exactly how much you will be paying to borrow money, the Truth in Lending Act (TILA) requires lenders to clearly disclose the annual percentage rate (APR), payment schedule, and the total amount of all payments. You can also use an online calculator from websites like bankrate.com or calculator.net to help determine the total amount you will ultimately pay.

While the truth in lending standards apply to credit cards and other revolving lines of credit, the variable nature of repayment makes it very difficult to forecast exactly what it will cost. Much like the Rule of 72 can help you understand how your money can grow, it can also be used in reverse to help you understand how much you could be paying to borrow money.

A credit card with a 20% interest rate (72÷20=3.6) would see the balance double in 3.6 years if no payments were made. Of course, credit card issuers would never let you go without making any payments and federal rules require that minimum payments cover at least the accrued interest (typically 2% of the balance per month) to avoid negative amortization, so the balance in this example would not actually double. It is feasible however, that if only minimum payments were made toward this balance, every 3.6 years you would have paid an amount equal to the outstanding balance.

When it comes to buying a house or a car, the price could easily be greater than what you can reasonably save up for or pay out of your normal cash flow. In these cases, the cost to borrow is simply the cost of admission. Without credit, you would not be able to make this purchase. This comes down to a true assessment of whether or not you really need this purchase. If, on the other hand, you are using credit to *avoid the pain* of paying, you are making the problem worse, and ultimately more painful.

The cost of college is a great way to understand the three different ways to pay. According to the National Center for Education Statistics, the average cost of a 4-year degree across all institutions in 2016 was a little over $26,000.[1] Interestingly, that seems to highlight our preference for paying after the fact and our willingness to indulge in a little extra spending when credit is made available. Information collected by The Institute for College Access & Success showed that two out of three (65 percent) college seniors who graduated from public and private nonprofit colleges in 2017 had student loan debt. These borrowers owed an average of $28,650.[2] As of this writing, debt.com listed the average student loan interest rate at 4.66%, so if these loans were paid off on the typical 10-year schedule, with no deferments, forbearance, or income-based repayment modifications, the total amount paid for a bachelor's degree would be close to $38,000.

Would you rather pay $26,000, something less than $26,000, or $38,000 for a four-year degree?

Debt as leverage

The things we buy can either appreciate or depreciate in value. When you consider this along with the cost to borrow, you can get a much clearer picture of what you're really getting for your money.

Some successful people love debt and try to use it to their advantage. (*Rich Dad, Poor Dad* [3] author Robert Kiyosaki, for one.) If you have the discipline to identify the appropriate uses of debt and apply that to purchase only things that are *assets* and/or produce income, then it can work for you.

The cornerstone of debt, or leverage, as a strategy is to buy assets that you believe will appreciate at a greater rate than what it will cost you to borrow. Or, if the asset produces an income, you could capture a spread between the income it produces and the cost to create positive cash flow. By using credit to pay for things that appreciate in value or produce income, you are simply forfeiting a portion of your gain.

If you are borrowing to buy a house, you can reasonably anticipate some level of long-term appreciation because in general there are limited homes and lots of people to buy them. You also benefit from owning an asset that can be rented and potentially produce income. At the very least, you get the utility of living in your house, which, given our earlier discussion on shelter as a basic need, you would have provided for yourself anyway.

A vehicle, however, typically depreciates in value, and over time becomes more expensive to maintain. If you finance it, then by the time you pay off the loan, you may have an asset that is worth significantly less than the total amount paid. You still benefit from owning a vehicle that can get you where you want to go, but the cost of that utility is represented in the difference between the reduced value and the total amount paid. The depreciation, or loss of value, you experience is essentially compounded by the cost to borrow, and you have to decide if you're getting your money's worth.

Borrowing money might be your only option when it comes to buying a vehicle, and much like shelter it ranks right up there at the top of the list of basic necessities. It is not an inappropriate use of credit, but it's not a great use of leverage.

The brand, type, features, and quality are all part of what borrowed money allows you to get. Leverage allows you to buy more vehicle than you probably can afford otherwise. If your car buying experience starts off with what payment you can afford, you might want to rethink how much you're willing to spend.

There's a lot more risk in being leveraged beyond owning an asset that can depreciate in value. As we all know too well from the crash of 2008, even homes don't always appreciate. With leverage you are obligating yourself to a stream of payments that can easily overwhelm your budget.

While leverage can potentially multiply the growth of money, or allow you to buy more than you can otherwise afford, people tend to use debt to buy consumables—things that give them instant gratification with little to show for it later. If you are using credit to buy single-use items or experiences, you're just spending money you don't have. You'll need to ask yourself if you have the discipline to use debt only for appropriate purposes.

Debt inflates our perceived spending power

If we're pursuing the objective of financial freedom by keeping our spending below our means, debt can become a major roadblock. Financial freedom assumes that we know our true financial resources. Debt artificially inflates what we believe we have in spending power.

Say you have an annual income of $60,000 but are lured by access to more capital in the form of $20,000 in available credit. You may perceive $80,000 as your total available resources. Even if your needs are at $65,000, the debt gives you an illusion of more wiggle room. Because we have this illusion, it tends to give us a feeling of *less* stress when we first use debt. As described in Chapter 3, you avoid the "pain" from the purchase and gain instant gratification.

But what happens once you begin using credit? If you didn't have enough money to fulfill your needs before, what is going to change that will allow you to meet your needs *and* pay back the amount you borrowed? You're now building a debt mountain with an Everest-like degree of difficulty to climb because you're already living at or above your means.

According to the "2017 U.S. Household Credit Card Debt Study" by NerdWallet, the average household carries $15,654 in credit card debt, an increase of eight percent from 2016.

Assuming a favorable interest rate of 13.99 percent, if that average $15,654 in credit card debt is paid off with only minimum payments, it will take 377 months (more than 31 years!) It would cost you more in additional interest— $17,762.86—than your original purchases (Bankrate Credit Card Calculator). And that's if you never spend another dollar on your cards.

When you've exhausted that credit source, suddenly you're maxed out. You're back to making and spending $60,000, but now the illusion of more spending power is gone. You've added the stress and cash drain of debt payments, and at some point you can't get more credit.

Also, beware of "buy-now-and-pay-no-interest-until…" offers. These are designed to give you the same false sense of more accessible resources, so you can afford it now and pay later. Of course, a hefty interest rate will kick in if you don't pay it on time, to the benefit of the finance company.

The credit trap

It's important not to feel financially "dumb" or abnormal if you've fallen into debt. We've all fallen for it. The only way we can avoid it is to be aware that credit cards and revolving credit are tactics being used against us.

The motivation to get you to take on credit may have been to sell you something you couldn't afford, but the goal of the creditor is to keep maintaining your debt to provide them with a continuous stream of income payments. As we have already covered, minimum payments are not meant to pay off debt, they are meant to keep you in debt.

Looking at just one month—May 2017—credit card issuers mailed 306 *million* card offers to people like us. Zero percent offers to "buy now and pay nothing for a limited time" or to transfer your debt to a new lender were the top most-mailed offers. That's according to Credit-Suisse, which tracks such things with its "U.S. Card Sector Review." Though mail offers are declining slightly, according to the report, card companies are just shifting tactics to more digital offers.

Lenders are not expending that kind of marketing effort without the expectations of profitable returns coming straight from your pocket to theirs. The data they use to identify their target consumers comes directly from your credit score. They see a number that tells them how likely you are to make your payments, and they practically beg you to unlock the spending potential your credit score has been able to provide.

Admit the problem

If you struggle with credit card debt, be careful not to become like the alcoholic who hasn't admitted the problem yet. Even if you feel like your spending is under control, don't allow yourself to live in denial about how harmful credit card debt is.

Most people generally have the feeling that at any point they can fix their situation. We tell ourselves, "I could pay all this off with a tax refund or a bonus." Or we justify a credit card balance because we have enough money in savings to cover the debt. Whether it's an extreme case with multiple cards maxed out to the credit limit or even just maintaining a balance that is outside your ability to pay off, carrying credit card debt is preventing you from achieving financial freedom.

Consider a scenario where you have $5,000 in your savings account while also carrying a $5,000 balance on your credit card. The interest you receive for your deposit is probably less than 1%, or $50, for an entire year. The credit card balance on the other hand, if the interest rate was 12%, would cost you $50 per month. You are effectively paying the bank to hold your cash, while you use theirs. They get a steady stream of income, you get the illusion of a cash safety net, or the belief that you are living within your means. In this scenario, however, you are broke. But, instead of just being broke and using your $5,000 savings to settle your debt, you are paying the bank $50 a month. What else could you use that money for?

To this point, we've covered the reasons why we are where we are. Admittedly, we've taken the Mr. Miyagi path in the chapters so far, but we needed to lay some ground work and introduce concepts that will help you be more successful—some "wax on, wax off" fundamentals, if you will.

For your plan to work, you have to make changes in your financial habits and outlook. In the next chapter, we'll look at how to create a budget, set your goals, and begin to work towards a balance between what you have and what you need.

Chapter Notes

1) "National Center for Education Statistics, Fast Facts: Tuition costs of colleges and universities,"
https://nces.ed.gov/fastfacts/display.asp?id=76

2) "Student Debt and the Class of 2017," The Institute for College Access & Success,
https://ticas.org/sites/default/files/pub_files/student_debt_and_the_class_of_2017_nr.pdf

3) *Rich Dad Poor Dad*; Robert T. Kiyosaki with Sharon L. Lechter, CPA; Warner Books, 1997/1998

6: Changing Our Behavior

"Our goals can only be reached through a vehicle of a plan, in which we must fervently believe, and upon which we must vigorously act. There is no other route to success."
——*Pablo Picasso*

Our cognitive biases and subconscious desires get us into trouble. Mental accounting, stress, and confusing our wants with needs put us in a place we don't want to be. It's almost as if we've inverted Maslow's hierarchy of needs. We've prioritized social belonging and esteem *wants* over safety and security *needs*. We've taken on debt to buy things we don't really need, threatening our ability to sustain ourselves, much less find contentment and financial freedom. We're ready for a change.

In our script scenario, we're at the second turning point when a change of plans is exactly what we need. The first act in our script has been about why we are where we are with our finances. The second act is about making changes and implementing a plan for reaching our goals.

If we want to rewrite our script to achieve financial freedom, we must commit to tracking our spending, re-evaluate our wants and our needs, and put diligent thought into our purchases.

You need to create a budget. One that you can stick to and that accounts for everything that is important to you: your lifestyle, your future, and the balance between what you need and what you have.

Rewriting your script, however, is as much about making changes as it is about understanding the script you have already been living.

Your story to this point, whether you realize it or not, has been pretty well documented. Pay stubs, account statements, and tax filings have all laid out what you make, what you spend and where you're headed. These personal financial statements are similar to the fundamental pieces of information used to analyze large companies or even small, local businesses down the street. A *balance sheet* (assets - liabilities) and a *cash flow statement* (income - expenses) tell the story of what you have, what you owe, what comes in, what goes out, and ultimately what's left over when it's all said and done.

Creating your plan

You might have a pretty good idea of where you would like to be financially. The truth is, most financial goals fall into one of only three categories: get caught up, get ahead, or live within your means. Identifying your goals is an important step, and something this chapter can help you do. But after setting your goals, the most critical part is having a plan to accomplish them.

It's okay if you're not the planning type. It doesn't have to be complicated. You need to figure out only a few key pieces of information to get headed in the right direction. Where are you now? Where do you want to be? When do you want to be there?

We'll follow these steps to get on track:

1. Calculate your *net worth* to know if you need to catch up or get ahead.
2. Understand your *cash flow* by identifying your actual income, tracking your current spending to see where

your money has been going, and identifying your necessary versus discretionary expenses.

3. Identify and set realistic *goals* that are important to you.

4. *Prioritize and compromise* between your goals and your current spending.

5. Create your *ideal budget* that enables you to accomplish your goals in the time frame you set.

Unexpected expenses will inevitably come up, and you'll need to change and adjust. That's okay too. When you apply this process, you are in control of your priorities. You decide between the goals you set, the resources you want to allocate to them, and the time it will take you to accomplish them.

Your balance sheet – finding your personal net worth

The difference between *gross* and *net* is a matter of subtracting what should not be counted as an asset. If I borrowed $1 million from the bank, could I say that I was a millionaire? If I looked only at the gross amount, I would not be seeing the whole picture. If I subtracted the $1 million outstanding loan from my gross assets, I would see a much more accurate reflection of my true worth.

To calculate your net worth, simply add up what you have (assets) and subtract what you owe (liabilities). The resulting amount can be either positive or negative but knowing the dollar amount will help you set your goals, to either catch up or get ahead.

Assessing the value of your assets can be tricky. Some asset values can be easily defined. Your checking or savings accounts along with the cash you keep under your mattress are worth what they're worth. While investment accounts and retirement savings may fluctuate with the market, the underlying securities are generally *liquid* and values update daily.

Other assets, however, like your home, car, or personal property, would need to be sold to realize their value. The length of time it could take as well as the cost to sell these assets make them *illiquid* and make it a little harder to accurately measure their value. When adding up illiquid assets as a part of your net worth, remember the endowment effect and that most of the things you own will likely not sell for what you think they are worth. For these assets it can help to seek professional resources like a realtor, car dealer, or collectables appraiser to identify an accurate valuation.

Keep in mind that it doesn't do you much good to overinflate your net worth by adding up lots of illiquid assets. Other than items with significant value that you normally see for sale in secondary markets, it's probably best to leave them out of your calculation. A good rule of thumb is that if it wasn't valuable enough to insure it against loss, then it's probably not worth considering an asset of any value.

If you own your own business, especially one that owns assets or has attempted to borrow money, you are probably well aware of balance sheets and cash flow statements. You should account for your ownership interest on your personal balance sheet. But, again, to avoid overinflating your net worth, list only the net value of your ownership interest in the business.

Liabilities and debt are a little easier to add up. When you owe money, the bank, business, or person you owe money to probably puts some effort into reminding you exactly how much you owe and when it is due. Go through your statements to list and add up your outstanding debts to find your total liabilities. If you are the one who is owed money from someone else—referred to as a receivable in accounting—you can list that under your assets.

Use the following table to list your assets and liabilities and find your net worth.

Net Worth

Assets		Liabilities	
Bank Accounts	$ _____	Credit Cards	$ _____
Investments	$ _____	Loans	$ _____
Real Estate	$ _____	Mortgages	$ _____
Personal Property	$ _____	Student Loans	$ _____
Business (net value)	$ _____	Other Debt	$ _____
Total Assets	$ _____	**Total Liabilities**	$ _____
NET WORTH (Total Assets - Total Liabilities)		(+ / -) $ _____	

Figure 6.1

Your cash flow – evaluating your income and expenses

Now that you have a better understanding of your net worth, the next step is to look at your *cash flow*, or, more specifically, what comes in and what goes out.

Income can be ordinary earned income (made from a job or self-employment) or passive income (made from investments, real estate, or business ownership). Your income can be fixed or variable, steady or infrequent. No matter how you make your money, how often you get paid, or how much you make, you need to know what you're working with if you want to establish goals, prioritize expenses or implement changes.

To prepare your cash flow statement, you'll need to add up your sources of income and subtract all your expenses. Much like finding your net worth, the result can be negative or positive. Evaluating your income and expenses will ultimately reveal if you are living within your means or spending more than you make.

Income vs available income

It's not always easy to know exactly what you make. While fixed salaries are typically steady, hourly or commission-based pay can vary or be unpredictable. Your income may even dramatically change from month to month or year to year. Regardless of income stability or amount, the most important number is what's available for you to spend. Before you can establish goals and create a budget, you need to know what you're working with.

For W-2 employees there are probably automatic deductions before you ever see them. These deductions typically include taxes and any benefits like health insurance and employer-sponsored retirement savings.

If you're self-employed or don't have the convenience of a payroll service, it's a little more complicated. You still need to account for income taxes as well as Social Security and Medicare. You should consult a tax professional if you feel you need additional assistance in setting aside the appropriate amount of taxes for your income level.

The difference between your gross pay and your net pay can be significant, and it can be a source of frustration when you see how those deductions add up. Take an example of someone who makes $75,000 per year. After taxes and other payroll deductions like health insurance and retirement savings, the take-home pay can easily be about two-thirds of that amount. All of this person's lifestyle and spending decisions will need to be based on the remaining $50,000.

The following table can help you track and account for deductions from all your income sources.

Available Income			
Gross Income			
Source	_____	_____	_____
Amount	$ _____	$ _____	$ _____	$ _____
Withholding & Payroll Deductions			
Federal Income Tax	$ _____	$ _____	$ _____	$ _____
State Income Tax	$ _____	$ _____	$ _____	$ _____
Soc. Sec. & Medicare	$ _____	$ _____	$ _____	$ _____
Medical, Dental, RX Ins.	$ _____	$ _____	$ _____	$ _____
Life & Disability Insurance	$ _____	$ _____	$ _____	$ _____
Retirement/401k Savings	$ _____	$ _____	$ _____	$ _____
All Other	$ _____	$ _____	$ _____	$ _____
Net Income	$ _____	$ _____	$ _____	$ _____
TOTAL AVAILABLE INCOME (Take-home pay)	$ _____		

Figure 6.2

This exercise may help you understand exactly where your gross income goes before it hits your bank account. You can also simply fill in the "Net Income" field with your take-home pay if these deductions are withheld automatically.

There is a good reason for automatically deducting these obligations. Since there are serious consequences for not paying your taxes or health insurance premiums, automatic deductions protect you from not doing it yourself.

In the same way, what other expenses or obligations do you have that come with serious consequences if they go unpaid? Mortgages or rent, car payments, and credit cards, as well as groceries and utility bills are just a few examples. Thinking about your bills along these lines is one way to help you classify some of your necessary versus discretionary spending. It also points out the reason why we need to stop basing our lifestyles on what we make, but instead on what is available after accounting for our needs and obligations.

Variable income

Most of your expenses are probably not variable, but when your income is, it can put a lot of stress on your budget and lead you toward reliance on credit to even out the dips. Rather than let the ups and downs of your paycheck change your lifestyle and behavior, you can take control. There are multiple ways to manage variable income and you must decide what works best for you.

The simplest method is to base your budget off the low end of your income range. Review your last 12 months to identify the month with the least amount of income, then design your lifestyle around that amount. Depending on the degree to which your income varies, this method can be very restrictive and not a true representation of the lifestyle you can likely afford. Commission-based incomes or incomes that pay infrequently probably won't work well with this method.

If that's the case for you, you'll likely need to base your budget on an average monthly income. Think back to Chapter 2 and the sugarcane farmers from the research by Shafir and Mullainathan. These farmers were paid only once a year when they harvested their crops and needed the surge of income to last until the following year's harvest. Establishing a monthly average and effectively rationing money from the good months to cover expenses during periods of lower income is the best way to live a stable lifestyle with unstable cashflow.

Again, review your last 12 months of income to get as accurate an average as possible. You might also consider either applying a bell curve by dropping the highest and lowest months from consideration or, for a more conservative approach, just eliminate your highest income months from the calculation.

Now let's look at the other half of the cash flow equation—expenses.

Tracking your spending

Be prepared to invest significant time into this part of the plan. The more in-depth you can get, the better the information you'll have to make decisions.

Your bank may offer some online tools to help you categorize your spending. Or, if you are comfortable sharing your banking information with a third-party website, you can use sites like mint.com or everydollar.com. While those resources are helpful, it may be most beneficial to go through your bank and credit statements line-by-line and track your spending yourself. This way, you may see where some unnecessary purchases have added up to a significant amount.

At the very least, you'll want to look at the last 90 days of statements to figure out an accurate average for some of your variable expenses. It's also important to note that some expenses occur only once or twice a year and you don't want to be surprised when they come due. If you really want to dig deep and get a crystal-clear picture of every expense, look at one year's worth of expenses so you can better prepare or save up for sporadic or infrequent bills.

Look for expenses that occur regularly every month. These may be fixed costs that never change, such as subscriptions or internet and cable TV services, or they may be variable, recurring expenses like a utility bill that you can average over several months. When you start to dig into your expenses, the underlying information we want to uncover is which expenses are fixed or variable, recurring or intermittent, and where you've drawn the line between needs and wants.

Your spending should break down into basic categories like the ones listed here:

Income Taxes (not withheld)	Transportation
Debt Payments	Utilities
Savings	Communications
Housing	Health
Food	Entertainment
Miscellaneous	Family

As you can imagine, there are a lot of different expenses that fit into these categories. Everyone has a unique spending situation and these categories are intended to keep this process as simple as possible. The following table includes some of the typical expenses that fit within these categories and can be downloaded as a PDF from www.thebalancingactbook.com or you can make a copy of the worksheet from the appendix in the back of this book.

Monthly Expenses

Income Taxes (not withheld)		Transportation	
Federal	$	Auto Loans, Leases	$
State	$	Registration Fees	$
Soc. Sec & Medicare	$	Fuel & Maintenance	$
Other Taxes	$	Auto Insurance	$
Debt Payments		Parking & Tolls	$
Credit Cards	$	Taxi & Transit	$
Personal Loans	$	Other	$
Student Loans	$	**Utilities**	
Other Debts	$	Gas & Electricity	$
Savings		Water	$
Emergency	$	Trash	$
Retirement	$	Other	$
College	$	**Communications**	
Other	$	Phone, TV, Internet	$
Housing		Cell Phone	$
Mortgage, Rent	$	Media Subscriptions	$
Maintenance & Repairs	$	Other	$
Property Tax & Insurance	$	**Health**	
Homeowners Fees	$	Insurance	$
Furnishings & Décor	$	Medical, Dental, Rx	$
Other	$	Other	$
Food		**Entertainment**	
Groceries	$	Vacation & Travel	$
Dining Out	$	News & Magazines	$
Other	$	Concerts, Theater, Arts	$
Miscellaneous		Other	$
Tithe, Charity & Donations	$	**Family**	
Hobbies	$	Education & Tuition	$
Clothing	$	Daycare & Babysitting	$
Dry Cleaning & Laundry	$	Lessons, Sports, Activities	$
Cleaning / Housekeeping	$	Memberships	$
Lawn & Garden	$	Alimony / Child Support	$
Other	$	Other	$
TOTAL MONTHLY EXPENSES		$	

Figure 6.3

You can also create your own custom spreadsheet. But try to fit your expenses into these basic categories to stay organized and not get distracted by too many expense classifications. The miscellaneous category can act as a "catch all" for those expenses that just don't seem to fit anywhere else.

While this process is designed to break down your spending into monthly increments, you will want to account for expenses that don't necessarily occur every month. Auto insurance premiums, vacations, or special events might only come up once or twice a year.

When you come across these expenses, find the annual amount spent and divide by 12. This will allow you to keep track of infrequent expenses and account for them on a monthly basis. It might not necessarily encourage you to specifically set aside these dollars and save up for infrequent expenses, but it may prevent you from thinking you have more of your income available to spend in other areas of your budget.

Remember to also note which expenses are fixed and which are variable. This will help you budget for the potential range of your variable expenses. It will also help you identify areas in which you can cut back or implement better controls on spending if your goals require reducing your monthly expenses.

Once you list all your expenses and add them up, determine your monthly cash flow by subtracting your total current monthly expenses from your available monthly income. Remember, this number can be either negative or positive and will indicate if you are living at, below, or above your means.

Available Monthly Income
<u>- Total Monthly Expenses</u>
(+/-) Monthly Cash Flow

Your personal cash flow statement will tell you if you are operating at a loss or gain, or if you're breaking even, and while that's incredibly useful information, it only tells you where you are, not how to make it better. You will need to review your spending if you want to make changes to your cash flow. The first place to look is where you draw the line between your needs and your wants.

Necessary vs discretionary spending

This step requires you to go through your expenses and separate your necessary from your discretionary spending. This is why it's beneficial to go through your bank statements line-by-line when you're tracking, classifying, and categorizing your expenses. The easiest way to list and add up your necessary and discretionary expenses is to use the same categories you used to track your spending.

Look at each of your expenses and ask yourself a simple question, "Was this necessary?" While it's a yes or no question, there are always some gray areas. Don't get too caught up in justifying every expense as there will be time after you set your goals to prioritize your spending. You want to mark the expenses you consider to be needs, then the rest fall under discretionary.

Taxes and debt obligations are mandatory expenses and will need to be listed as necessary. Depending on your commitment to savings, this category can be either necessary or discretionary or some combination of both. As an example, you may consider retirement to be a necessity while saving toward next year's family vacation is a more discretionary objective.

Use the following table to break down your spending and find your necessary and discretionary totals. Some categories may include expenses that are automatically deducted from your paycheck like taxes or health insurance. To prevent counting these deductions twice, we will use the "Total Available Income" or "take-home pay" figure when comparing our expenses to our income. So, only include expenses that are not automatically deducted from your paycheck in your necessary versus discretionary analysis.

Necessary vs Discretionary Expenses

Spending Categories	Necessary	Discretionary
Taxes (not withheld)	$	$
Debts & Loans	$	$
Savings	$	$
Housing & Utilities	$	$
Food	$	$
Transportation	$	$
Health	$	$
Family	$	$
Entertainment	$	$
Miscelaneous	$	$
Total $		**Total** $

Figure 6.4

Add each column to find the totals for your necessary and discretionary expenses. By looking at your expenses this way, you can start to see areas where spending changes can improve your cash flow. Ultimately you want to break down your cash flow to understand how much is going toward necessary and discretionary expenses.

To do this, take your total necessary expense and subtract it from your available income. This will reveal your available discretionary income.

> Available Income
> - Total Necessary Expenses
> (+/-) Available Discretionary Income

If your available discretionary income is a negative number, that means your necessary expenses are eating up your entire budget. This can either be from overemphasizing your needs and where you draw the line between necessary and discretionary spending, or your needs truly exceed your income and you are living an unsustainable lifestyle. If the amount you are spending on discretionary expenses exceeds your available discretionary income, your cash flow analysis would indicate you are living beyond your means.

While adjusting your budget will probably start with your discretionary expenses, you may need to reevaluate your needs or make more significant changes to your lifestyle to free up available income and create positive cash flow.

Dividing your spending into necessary or discretionary expenses allows you to know where to start making budget changes to increase your cash flow. It also helps you understand how much of your income is potentially available for your goals.

If your cash flow is positive, then you have income to fund your goals. Changing your necessary or discretionary spending can increase the degree to which your cash flow is positive, potentially allowing you to put more toward your goals.

If your cash flow is negative, but you have money left over after covering your needs, then you can create positive cash flow by changing your discretionary spending. Again, depending on the degree to which you change your spending, you would potentially have some money left for your goals.

Identifying and setting goals

After tracking and categorizing your spending as either necessary or discretionary, it's time to start focusing on your goals. While the three most common budgeting goals are to get caught up, get ahead, or to simply spend less than you make, this is the time to think about what you want to accomplish.

Do you want to be debt free? Do you want to build your wealth so you can sustainably live a better lifestyle? Do you just want to live within your means and reduce the stress of not meeting what you consider to be your needs? Or, do you want all three?

Of the three goals, living comfortably within your means is the most significant. Getting caught up or getting ahead won't happen if you can't control your spending. The rate at which you will be able to accomplish either of those goals is completely dependent on the amount you have left after covering your expenses. If you master your budget and learn to live below your means, the other goals will work themselves out naturally.

If you have debt, and your goal is to pay it off, there are a number of strategies for getting that done. In Chapter 8, we'll cover those strategies and several options for accomplishing that goal. But all of that will be for nothing if you don't address and solve the problem that created that debt in the first place. The long-term solution is to learn to live comfortably within your means and not rely on debt to cover expenses that exceed your income. If you spend less than you make, you'll never need to use debt to finance your lifestyle spending.

If you want to build wealth, you'll need to have some extra income to set aside, and, again, that is only possible if you spend less than you make.

Living below your means is the foundation of financial freedom. By achieving this goal, you will inevitably achieve the other two.

Be aggressive but realistic in setting your goals

Jim Collins is well-known within the business community for his work as a researcher, author, and teacher of corporate leadership. In his book co-authored with Jerry Porras, *Built to Last: Successful Habits of Visionary Companies*[1], they wrote about a common theme that successful companies share: A big, hairy, audacious goal or BHAG (pronounced bee-hag).

A BHAG is a clear, compelling goal that allows effort to be sharply focused toward its achievement. Former President Kennedy's declaration to land on the moon and return safely, Microsoft's desire to see a computer on every desk and in every home, or Nike's goal to "crush Adidas" are just a few examples.

While these are all big goals and it would be easy to infer that successful organizations gained their success from declaring these BHAGs, this overlooks a very simple fact. You need the skills and the resources to achieve your BHAG, otherwise you are just wishing for something out of reach. This book was written to teach you the skills to spend within your means, but the resources (the money needed) to achieve your goals must come from you.

Starting with nothing and building a net worth of $10 million in the next ten years is certainly a big, hairy, audacious goal, and the material in this book can help with the skills necessary to achieve that goal. But, without the resources to back that up, it's probably not going to happen.

The important next step is to include both a dollar amount and a timeline for each goal. Without knowing when you will accomplish your goal, it's just a wish. When you set a time frame, it's an important check to be sure that what you want to do is practical. Do you really have the dollars in income to pay off debt, build savings, or achieve whatever your goal is, by the date you specify?

What we don't want is for you to get discouraged when you start down a path and find you can't achieve that goal. Realistic goals prevent falling back into old habits, putting yourself further behind what you want to accomplish, and maybe giving up altogether.

So, identify realistic goals and a realistic way to achieve each goal by a specified date. Here are some examples:

- Pay off $7,000 in credit card debt in 36 months.
- Save $10,000 for your child's college education in the next five years.
- Contribute $5,000 every year to an IRA for retirement.
- Create a $1,000 emergency fund in the next six months.

Getting out of "the hole" doesn't mean just getting out of debt

People tend to assume that "being in the hole" implies a negative number. The most common thought is to imagine being thousands in debt, and figure that getting back to even would get you "out of the hole." But the truth is that you can be debt free and still be in the hole when you look at the big picture of your new goals and financial plan.

For example, between now and when you retire you may want to build a certain amount of positive savings. If your goal is to have $1 million for retirement and you have 20 years until that day, then there is a line that can be drawn between what you have saved already and the amount you will need. If you end up with less money than you need to meet your goal, then you are in the hole relative to your plan.

So the hole is not always debt, but how far you are behind the line that defines the necessary path between achieving your ultimate goal and when you want to have it accomplished.

Prioritize and compromise

Now that you've had a chance to track your spending and separate your needs from your wants, you are better equipped to re-evaluate where you're allocating your money. This is the most likely way to uncover the resources necessary to accomplish your goals. As pointed out in the beginning of the book, making more money is not something you can always count on, and because of the added stress of chasing after more, it's not a recommended approach. The focus here is to work with the dollars you have now.

If, in going through this budget exercise, you have some spending that doesn't fit the basic categories, you probably have a propensity to spend on things you don't need. Circle back to the previous chapters to review how to make decisions and how to make changes to meet your needs within your means. A serious look at your needs and your wants and reevaluating where you are allocating your money is the most likely way to uncover ways to live below your means and find money to pursue your goals.

Remember that this isn't about depriving yourself or living a minimalist lifestyle. Instead, it is about a longer-term perspective that includes the future for you and your family. Your answers to the Chapter 1 Self-Assessment probably revealed some areas of your life where you want change. Keep that in mind as you prioritize items in your budget.

Expenses you've listed in the "discretionary" sections of the budget are good places to look first:

- Everyone needs housing, but if it was as simple as checking the box for "roof over your head" then we'd all be happy. Looking a little deeper, are you paying the right amount of money for the shelter benefits you're receiving?

- Transportation needs generally require a car or two. But think again about your choice of vehicle. Go back to Chapter 3 if you need to think about what's motivating you and if you could reduce your transportation expense.

- Food starts with *where* you shop. Do you go to a store just for the prestige? Another store may fulfill your food need for less. If you're up for a little more effort to save on your groceries, check the Resources section at the end of this book, or read books like *Live Your Life for Half the Price*[2] by Mary Hunt.

- Eating out may be just about habits rather than an experience or enjoyment. If you'd rather not cut back on frequency, choice of where you go could trim expenses here.

- Memberships at Planet Fitness go unused by half its members, according to the podcast "Money Planet." A *USA Today* story[3] says two-thirds of all gym memberships go unused. Check to see if your memberships are delivering the value intended.

You've also set some important goals. There's satisfaction and financial freedom to be had in accomplishing those goals. As you'll see from the personal stories in Chapter 10, you'll most likely be happy you made these changes and not miss anything you might have to give up.

When you prioritize and compromise you can maximize the money you have left over each month, and over the course of a year that can really add up. Imagine having $5,000 or $10,000 left over between your income and your spending that you can control and manage to meet your goals. The potential payoffs could be building personal wealth, retiring earlier, paying cash for vacations and other discretionary luxuries, no longer feeding the debt industry, and reaching financial freedom.

Create your ideal budget

Now that you've tracked your spending, analyzed your cash flow, set goals, and prioritized your spending, it's time to create and commit to your ideal budget. Since you've examined your expenses and defined your necessary and discretionary boundaries, you can incorporate that into your planned budget. Use the same worksheet you used to track your spending, only this time put down what you *plan* to spend in the corresponding expense categories. Fill the worksheet out once with only necessary expenses, and a second time with discretionary expenses.

Looking at your budget as two separate pieces allows you to clearly account for your needs and identify exactly what is left for your discretionary spending. Beyond simply identifying your available discretionary income, you can now decide how you want to allocate that money.

When you are prioritizing and compromising, you're not only deciding between what constitutes a need and a want, you're deciding between achieving your goals and your immediate desires to consume. You are in control of where your money is going, not regretfully spending on things you didn't really want or couldn't really afford.

Creating financial freedom in the balance between what you need and what you have means defining exactly what you need, and then using what's left to provide for what you want. By using this budgeting process, you can ensure that your true needs are covered, you have a path toward achieving your goals, and you are empowered to use your money on what is most important to you.

Changing your financial behavior starts with understanding where you are and identifying where you want to be. But achieving your goals will take more than simply wanting to achieve them. Whether you are trying to live within your means, get caught up, or get ahead, the ability to achieve these goals will depend on your ability to implement and stick to your plan. Beyond creating a budget, let's look at strategies and methods that can help you realize the goals you want to achieve.

Chapter Notes

1) *Built to Last, Successful Habits of Visionary Companies*, Jim Collins, Harper Business, 2011

2) *Live Your Life for Half the Price*, Mary Hunt, Revell, 2015

3) "Is Your Gym Membership A Good Investment?" USA Today, 2016, https://www.usatoday.com/story/money/personalfinance/2016/04/27/your-gym-membership-good-invest

7: Maintaining Balance

*"Annual income twenty pounds, annual
expenditure nineteen six, result happiness.
Annual income twenty pounds, annual
expenditure twenty pounds ought and six,
result misery."*
— David Copperfield, by Charles Dickens

While there are typically only three different categories of
goals, maintaining a balanced budget is the most crucial. As
mentioned in the previous chapter, without achieving this goal
and mastering the skills necessary to stay on track, you will
have a hard time accomplishing your other goals. Maintaining
your balance is no more than living below your means, simple
as that. Once you've found that balance, then you can move
on to paying off debt or getting ahead.

At this point you should have tracked your spending and
identified where your money has been going. The prioritize-
and-compromise exercise allowed you to review your needs
and your wants and set your goals for allocating between
necessary and discretionary spending. You may have been able
to identify where false perceptions or irrational mental
accounting has led you to build an unsustainable list of needs.

Making it easier to fulfill our needs by "lowering the bar"

As our list of needs increases, our financial stress increases. We
feel the weight of needing to generate greater and greater

income to sustain our lifestyles. On the other hand, if we can determine which *needs* may actually be *wants*, we can strike them from the list. In this way, we can lower the financial bar and limit our needs to a much more achievable level.

Lowering your needs bar is another way to build a margin between your income and your spending. The greater the margin, the less stress you'll experience. Your pool of discretionary income will grow, giving you more options when allocating your money toward your future and other things that matter most to you.

When you plan ahead for discretionary wants, you can treat them as rewards rather than needs. You can feel pleasure and satisfaction by indulging in the extra, without the stress and worry that it has jeopardized your ability to provide what you really need.

After creating your budget and setting your goals, you may be motivated and ready to get going. But temptations can continue to hinder your progress. It may be easy to simply rely on discipline at first, but over time that can wear down and leave you susceptible to the challenges that got you where you are today. Let's look at a couple of strategies that can keep you on track by either enabling good behaviors or preventing bad ones.

Using mental shortcuts for good

You may be familiar with stories or examples of criminals who join law enforcement to help catch other criminals. In the movie *Catch Me If You Can*[1], based on a true story, Leonardo DiCaprio plays legendary con artist Frank Abagnale Jr. Abagnale posed as an airline pilot, doctor, and lawyer while forging millions of dollars in checks, all before he turned 20 years old! To get away with his crimes, he studied every detail of paper checks and how they are processed through the banking system.

After he is caught, rather than go to prison, the mastermind turns to a new life fighting crime for the FBI. He uses his encyclopedic knowledge of checks and banking as a positive force against the bad guys.

What if, in the same way, we could turn our new knowledge about how we make financial mistakes to our advantage? We've unwittingly been under the influence of mental accounting and heuristics, and we also know that our minds will continue to take these shortcuts. How can we use these shortcuts for good?

It's important to understand that the reason our mind uses these shortcuts in the first place is to simplify the decision-making process and give us an edge. By recognizing our natural tendencies and where these heuristics fall short, we can make them work for us instead of against us.

Relativity – understand the time it takes to earn what you spend

You make comparisons when gauging the value of one item relative to another. A great example of relativity comes from one of my favorite movies, *Crocodile Dundee*. When Mick visits New York, he and his girlfriend Sue are approached by a would-be thief wielding a knife. When Sue encourages Mick to give up his wallet because the robber has a knife, he responds, "That's not a knife." Then, brandishing his own, much-larger knife, he quips, "That's a knife." The bad guys run away and relativity has saved the day.

Like Crocodile Dundee's knife or the significance of savings relative to the original price, we naturally make determinations about value and whether we are getting our money's worth through relativity. If we know that our minds are hard wired to use this information to appraise value, how can we use that to our advantage?

Think beyond the monetary value and ask yourself a more existential question, "What is my time worth?" In the book *Your Money Or Your Life*[2], Vicki Robin introduces a strategy to think of "cost" in terms of the time it would take to earn that amount of money.

Money is the medium used in exchange for goods and services, but it takes time and effort to earn it. You're spending a precious resource that you can never get back in exchange for money that allows you to consume. Consume less, and you will need less money. Then you can use that time for more meaningful pursuits.

Take your *actual income*, which you calculated in the last chapter, and divide it by the number of hours it took you to earn that amount. If you want to get specific, divide it again, by 60, to get down to the minute. Here's an example of someone who works 40 hours a week or an average of 173 hours per month and has an after-tax-and-deduction take-home pay of $6,000 a month:

$6,000 ÷ 173 = $34.68 per hour, $34.68 ÷ 60 = $0.58 per minute

Is that $100 pair of shoes worth three hours of your life? You can also apply this to the recurring expenses you pay every month and ask yourself the same question. A $2,000 mortgage would be equal to 57 hours and 28 minutes of work every single month. That cost would represent a significant portion of your time and your life. Is it worth it? Are you happy with what you are getting for your time? If not, this may be an area in which you could consider making a lifestyle change.

Affect – know what you're missing for a quick purchase buzz

By now you are aware of how much your mind is influenced by feelings, and how we use those feelings to determine if a purchase is worth it or not. Unfortunately, because of our ability to recall positive feelings from immediate gratification rather than negative feelings from overspending, our gut instinct tricks us into unnecessary consumption. The great thing about this heuristic is that it works for positive and negative feelings. You just need to better connect your short-term spending choices with the long-term negative feelings that stress and living above your means can create.

When you tracked your spending as the first step in creating a budget, you may have noticed that little, insignificant purchases added up over time to equal large amounts of money. A $4 cup of coffee might not seem like it's going to break the bank, but three times a week for a year and you're talking $624.

Look at an average week of spending and track how many small purchases you make under $20. Add them up and compare that to the total amount of discretionary dollars you have available on a weekly basis. The grand total might be a little more painful than each individual purchase.

It's not just small purchases adding up that create negative feelings about overspending. Big purchases do too. Marketers are always trying to influence your purchase decisions by associating positive feelings with their products and services. They highlight the benefits of their products and try to appeal to the pleasure of fulfilling your desires.

Remember this assessment question at the end of Chapter 1: Can you remember a purchase you thought would make you happy but instead caused you financial stress?

You're already weighing the emotional pros and cons of your spending decisions. To turn the affect heuristic to your advantage, simply give the negative emotions from overspending a fighting chance at saving you from making a spending mistake.

If you can't think of negative consequences that could come from a decision to spend, then think about other positive feelings you might give up. Look at your potential purchase as a trade-off between this and something else that brings you enjoyment. Would missing out on the happiness from some other purchase or activity be worth the happiness you are about to experience for this one?

Tap into the power of relativity, and ask yourself, "What sacrifice would I have to make, or what convenience would I have to do without to have this?" You might really enjoy that cup of coffee three times a week. You have budgeted the annual cost of $624 that it takes to afford this extra treat. How many weeks would you have to go without your coffee to experience the happiness associated with some new expense you are considering?

Mental accounting and compartmentalization –improve your accuracy

Budgeting in general is a form of compartmentalization. You naturally treat money differently based on how you earn it, and you treat it differently based on what it's intended for.

Dollars are compartmentalized in a constructive way when you set aside money for housing, car payments, insurance, utilities, and other ongoing expenses. Whether you've created a formal budget or if you've relied on mental accounting, you have probably set aside money for the expenses with the highest priority.

Creating a budget is beneficial, and clearly something that I am encouraging my readers to do. But our default condition is not having to write everything down or use spreadsheets to track and forecast every expense. We want to be able to handle it in our heads. So, at the very least, let's make it easy on ourselves.

Separating your necessary and discretionary income is a great way to compartmentalize your money. Since you already identified your necessary and discretionary expenses in Chapter 6, it should be easy to figure out how much goes into each bucket. If all of your needs and necessary expenses equal $4,000 per month and your after-tax take-home pay is $5,000, then you know you can spend the difference, or $1,000, every month.

This is the most basic form of budgeting. If you do nothing more than identify your necessary expenses and limited your discretionary spending to the difference between your needs and your income, then you have taken your first step toward realizing financial freedom.

The problem is that this is not very easy to do, and mental accounting makes it even harder. When we look only at our total income and forget to account for all our necessary expenses, mental accounting can lead us astray.

If you suddenly have the opportunity to spend money on something you really want and it costs $250, mental accounting might leave you thinking that amount is not very much relative to the total amount you bring home every month. Using the example above, $250 is only about 5 percent of a $5,000 monthly income. However, if you account for your necessary expenses and know the amount left over for discretionary spending, then you would be aware of exactly how much this cost would be relative to what you can afford. In this example, $250 would be 25 percent, or one quarter, of your entire month's discretionary spending. This is a much more significant amount of your budget than you originally thought.

By simply being cognizant of your necessary and discretionary spending and compartmentalizing your income, you allow yourself to still use mental accounting, but with much more accuracy.

Ulysses agreement

The Odyssey, Homer's epic poem about Ulysses (Odysseus), tells a story from Greek mythology about the dangerous Sirens. The Sirens were irresistible to all men, using their beautiful songs to lure ships close to their island where the vessels would crash on the sharp rocks, killing all who approached.

Ulysses wanted to hear the beauty of the songs without losing his ship and men. To do it, he prepared before sailing close to the island by having his men tie him to the mast of his ship and then protecting his crew by having them stuff wax into their ears. He ordered them not to change course or let him free from the ropes no matter what he might say or do, posting sword-bearing guards close by to stop him from altering his plans.

This was his agreement to ensure his survival in the end. He knew he would be driven insane in the moment of hearing the sirens, and he was. But through a pre-planned strategy that prevented him from succumbing to temptation, he protected his future-self.

Pretty dramatic, right? Yet we all hear the siren songs of temptation that threaten our long-term planning every day: "I want it. I deserve it. Everyone else is doing it…"

We know from Chapter 3 and the illusory superiority bias that we tend to be overconfident about our abilities. This especially applies to our ability to resist temptation. The key to implementing a Ulysses agreement is understanding your temptations and then creating barriers that prevent you from giving in to them.

Imagine late one night setting an alarm clock to wake up early the next morning. At 11 p.m. you are thinking through all the stuff you have to do the next day and what time you'll need to wake up to accomplish everything.

But at 5 a.m. you might have slightly different priorities when deciding between sleeping in and accomplishing the things on your to-do list. The temptation of the snooze button and its immediate benefits are now at odds with the greater goals of accomplishing the things you set out to accomplish the night before.

Placing the alarm clock far enough away that you must get out of bed to turn it off is one way to remove the option and prevent 5 a.m. foggy-minded and sleep-deprived you from making a decision that does not benefit wide-awake and fully-alert you.

We can be our own worst enemy when it comes to sabotaging our best efforts. Let's look at a way to take compartmentalization to the next level with a plan to protect yourself from yourself. The following are systems you can use to implement your own Ulysses agreement to help prevent your long-term plans from being undermined by your short-term desires.

Cash-based budgeting – cash is king

While credit cards give you the ability to spend money you don't have, debit and ATM cards enable easier access to the money you do have. This leads to easier spending.

Have you noticed the burden of debit card transaction costs primarily lie on the shoulders of the merchants you're trying to buy from? Some stores may limit debit card purchases under a certain dollar amount because the fees can make it unprofitable to accept that form of payment for small transactions. For the most part, merchants gladly accept card transactions because they benefit from the ease with which you are separated from your money.

By tapping into your desire to avoid pain, you may be less inclined to spend when it involves physically handing over cash to someone in exchange for goods and services. A cash-only system can also make you more aware of how much money you have available and can even help you prioritize purchases. Whether it's a trip to an ATM or a visit to the bank to withdraw cash, you'll be limited in the frequency or times you'll be able to get your hands on more money.

Remember the example from Chapter 4 about the paycheck-to-paycheck mentality? Much like the last gallon of gas in your car, introducing difficulty in refilling your wallet or purse with cash will make you more mindful of how you're spending your money.

One challenge with this system is that there's risk in dealing with potentially large amounts of cash. There's an element of safety in using debit or credit cards since you can call the bank to deactivate them should they be lost or stolen. Banks and credit card companies also typically protect you from loss if the cards are fraudulently used.

With cash, the risk of loss is on you. However, you can limit any loss by making regularly scheduled trips to the bank or ATM to withdraw smaller amounts. By carrying less at any given time, you ultimately protect yourself from overspending.

Cash also generally requires you to be physically present for the transaction, so online purchases or payments over the phone aren't easily facilitated with cash. That can be a good way to cut spending too. But if you need to use a card with a cash-based budgeting system, you still can. Just subtract the charged amount from your cash on hand, then make a trip back to the bank or ATM to deposit that amount into your account.

Envelope budgeting

Creating a budget and allocating your income toward a variety of different categories can help you live within your means.

While simply using cash can keep you from overspending, budgeting with cash can help keep your spending plan on track. Things don't always go as planned and putting a budget into practice can be difficult. Using an envelope budgeting system is one effective way to implement your budgeting strategy.

Envelopes allow you to compartmentalize your cash-based budget. The concept is simple. After deciding which categories you're going to allocate your spending toward, put that amount of cash in an envelope designated for that category. On payday, or the frequency of your choosing, head to the bank and withdraw the cash needed to fill your envelopes.

Typically, these envelopes are used to cover expenses that are somewhat variable and can be paid in cash. Groceries, restaurants, and entertainment, as well as savings goals like vacations or large purchases, are all categories where this system works well.

You'll still have fixed expenses, like car payments, rent or mortgage, as well as bills that are paid electronically or with checks. Consider your checking account to be the "master envelope" from which these expenses are paid and all other cash envelopes are filled.

With this separation, there is less temptation to take dollars from true needs to spend on discretionary purchases, and when each envelopes' dollars are gone, they're gone. No more spending in that category until the envelope is replenished.

You'll need to be disciplined to make this system work. When you allocate cash to an envelope, you must keep yourself from using it for anything other than that envelope's intended purpose. Borrowing from one envelope to fulfill a different need can lead to a cascading breakdown of the system, setting you right back to square one.

The foundation of envelope budgeting, or a cash-based budgeting system in general, is the restriction of available cash. The more difficult you make it to access cash, the less likely you are to spend it. Without the hard limitation on cash availability, you may find that having access to large amounts of cash can actually work against your savings efforts. You may even feel more inclined to spend on spontaneous purchases simply because the cash is available. If the convenience of carrying cash is going to enable you to spend, this might not be the best system for you. Or you may benefit from a slightly more stringent version of this system.

Gift card system

In a slight twist on the envelope system, gift cards can help you stay on budget and give to a worthwhile cause at the same time. Rather than stuffing cash into an envelope, buy gift cards for the categories you are allocating your spending towards. You then lock up that money for the sole purpose of fulfilling that category. It's much more restrictive than envelope budgeting because you can't simply "borrow" from one category and apply it to another. Gift cards for gas stations can only be used for gas, grocery stores for groceries, restaurants, entertainment…you get the picture.

You can also give back by purchasing your gift cards from your school, church, or other source, which then receives a percentage of the amount in the form of a rebate. Often called "Scrip" programs, ask if your school, sports program, or another non-profit important to you sells Scrip gift cards and you can stay on budget and do good at the same time.

Couponing

I have read a number of personal finance books, and it seems people fall into two camps on couponing: love it or hate it. Some people seem to love the idea of working to beat retailers at their discount game, while others think it's too much effort for the savings gained.

If you are willing to get "paid" in savings by investing a little time, take a look at the Appendix for a list of coupon sites and apps compiled by moneypantry.com in the article, "The 20 Best Coupon Sites."

Before we move on from coupons, beware of the "couponing mindset":

- Don't fall for product manufacturer's desire to get you to buy something new or additional beyond what you need.

- "Stocking up" on sale items only goes so far—don't let your pantry and/or garage become more heavily stocked than the supermarket shelves.

Used for good, coupons can help you save on items you already buy. To avoid spending money on what you don't need, stick to a list and wait for items you already buy to come on sale.

Pay yourself first

Apply your income to your savings goals and absolutely necessary spending needs first before any other expenses derail your efforts. There is a good reason why the government wants to take your income taxes right out of your paycheck: It is much easier to get money from someone who has it than someone who doesn't. Remember, we tend to spend right up to the limit of what is available, and in the case of collecting taxes, the government would prefer to collect what is owed before you have that opportunity. If we were all left to save up on our own and pay our taxes at the end of the year, there is a good chance that IRS agents would look less like accountants and more like bounty hunters.

This is the very same reason why you should be paying yourself first. If your money is not going toward your goals, then there is a good chance you will find something else to spend it on. By paying yourself first and setting aside money for your goals, you are creating a barrier that prevents you from spending on something less important.

There are many personal finance books that include this as a basic principle. One classic is from George S. Clason, called *The Richest Man in Babylon*.[3] The book is unique in weaving financial advice into a novel-format story and is certainly a personal favorite. The first among Clason's "Seven Cures for a Lean Purse," is to set aside 10 percent of income for yourself before paying anyone else.

When you take this approach, you are limiting the amount of money you have available to yourself for day-to-day expenses. When we trick our minds into believing we have less available, we adapt to less and learn to live on that amount.

Automate and separate

Separating your money into different accounts based on the intended use is one way to take compartmentalization to the next level. Maintaining multiple accounts allows you to better earmark funds for specific purposes and can keep you on track to achieve your goals.

Splitting your income into accounts assigned for necessary and discretionary spending is the best approach to staying on budget. By creating a barrier between these pools of money you prevent yourself from using funds earmarked for necessary purposes on discretionary expenses.

The most common arrangement, and what most banks offer, is simply a savings and a checking account. You can take this one step further by opening a separate checking and savings account at a different bank or institution. As a barrier, treat additional accounts as "hidden" and limit your access to them. When I say hidden, I mean hidden from your view. No checkbook, debit card, or credit card should be attached to these accounts.

The only way money can come out is for you to literally walk into a branch and ask for cash or a cashier's check. You may even consider feeding these funds into an investment or brokerage account, which typically takes a day or two to move money between institutions. That creates a time delay or "circuit breaker" between you and your money, which can be a valuable pause when you have the urge to spend.

Automating your budget prevents you from deviating from the already-established plan or intended purpose for your money. Most payroll services allow for deposits into multiple accounts, and once your money is there you can use bill-pay features and automatic transfers to further allocate money to where it needs to go.

When you tracked your spending in the last chapter you should have noted your recurring expenses. These are the bills or payments that you make every month. They might not be the same amount every month, but they're probably in the same ballpark. Examples of these expenses are mortgage or rent, car payments, insurance, phone, internet, cable, or any subscriptions or services you consider to be needs.

Use the account you set up as your necessary spending account to automatically pay these bills. It's very important to make sure that the amount you put in this account is enough to cover all expenses to be automatically deducted each month. Because some of those expenses may be variable, you should consider padding the account with more than one month's worth of expenses. This can be a great way to work on establishing emergency savings. (We will discuss this more in the next chapter.)

The amount left after covering your necessary expenses can go into your discretionary account. This will be the account that you use for day-to-day expenses, and any extra or unplanned spending. This should be the only account to which you allow yourself easy access with checks, debit cards, or account information saved to online shopping platforms.

In addition to maintaining separate accounts for your necessary and discretionary spending, you can use separate accounts for all your savings goals. If you participate in an employer-sponsored retirement plan like a 401(k), it is likely that you are already implementing this strategy. These approaches work for more than just long-term goals like retirement. You can apply them to short-term savings goals too.

When you combine the "pay yourself first" mentality with separate accounts and an automated budget, you enable yourself to act in your own best interest and make it easier to achieve your goals. By taking money directly out of your paycheck and applying it toward your goals, it's removed from your available income and you learn to live on what's left. Dividing this left-over money between your necessary and discretionary spending helps to ensure that your needs are met, and you have a defined limit on what is available for discretionary expenses.

However, just because you know your limit doesn't mean you will abide by it. Another barrier that can help you ration your spending and keep you within your self-imposed limit is the use of an allowance.

Weekly discretionary allowance

Many of our recurring expenses are billed monthly and that naturally leads us to break down our spending into monthly budgets regardless of how frequently we get paid. Yet the urge to satisfy your current-self at the expense of your future-self, and the tendency to use mental accounting to track and regulate your spending, makes it very difficult to manage money over such a relatively long period of time.

Let's say that each month you have $1,000 left for your discretionary budget. Because you're wired to discount the future value of something when presented with an immediate benefit (hyperbolic discounting), you may feel you have the full $1,000 at your disposal right now. As the month goes by and you're running low on money, you may be tempted to re-evaluate your goals, save less, or, even worse, fall back into using debt to cover your short-term desires.

Instead, set up your own Ulysses agreement by dividing your $1,000 into smaller $250 weekly payments. Rather than leave it to conscious action, set this payment up as an auto withdrawal from your necessary spending account into your discretionary spending account. This way you're sure to have just as much the last week of the month as the first. Even better, pay yourself each Monday and you'll probably end up spending less during the week so you have money for the weekend.

If a large expense comes up during the month that is greater than your weekly allowance, you can decide if you want to spend the money now and reduce the allowance available through the rest of the month. Much like the tradeoff we discussed when using the affect heuristic to your advantage, you can calculate the exact amount by which you would be decreasing your future weekly allowance to satisfy this large expense and decide if it's worth it.

Understanding the challenges that have led you to this point and applying what you've learned to change your ways are steps toward maintaining your balance. Implementing tangible budgeting strategies like a cash-based envelope system or maintaining separate and automated accounts can help you live below your means. There are other, less-tangible elements to maintaining a balanced budget and achieving financial freedom, and those come down to a frame of mind.

Resist adaptation

Remember the concept of the hedonic treadmill? In Chapter 1 we saw that psychologist Kahneman and economist Deaton found that we quickly adapt to rises in income, summing it up in the title of their paper: "High income improves evaluation of life but not emotional well-being."

Let's hope we all see plenty of pay raises during our careers. When those happy days come, it's a time to celebrate further progress toward our goals and a sustainable lifestyle. What we need to resist is the urge to ratchet up our lifestyle to spend all that we make.

Since we know that we'll soon lose any emotional boost that a raise brings, more money paid to us should not result in equal changes to how much we pay ourselves. Instead, allocate more funds to your goals: retirement, college savings, paying off debt, and charitable giving, to name a few. This is the time to be firmly connected to your future-self.

It is also true that behavioral psychologists have discovered the idea that smaller, "hedonic boosts" have a more lasting effect on our happiness. Dan Ariely again pops up in a joint study with Daniel Mochon and Michael I. Norton titled, "Getting off the hedonic treadmill, one step at a time: The impact of regular religious practice and exercise on well-being."[4]

Their recommendation? Rather than seeking major life events to find happiness, use everyday positive boosts to gain more lasting well-being. For their study, they surveyed attendees of places of worship, and found that the more regular the attendance, the happier those people reported being.

In a second study, they looked at other positive activities, like exercise and yoga. People regularly engaging in those activities also reported a cumulative positive impact on their well-being.

For you, how about the satisfaction of progress toward your goals, volunteering, or charitable giving as some of those ongoing positive boosts?

The media share stories of the unhappy rich and famous time after time. Those individuals obviously experienced some major successes that we would expect to bring them plenty of happiness. But, in these cases, our human nature naturally equalizes our state of well-being, then pushes us to the next big achievement. Instead, maybe we need to be looking at smaller, daily or weekly positive activities for us to gain true well-being and avoid constant striving for more.

Purchase flow chart

Another way to avoid the automatic actions of our minds is to take a more systematic approach to our spending decisions. Keep it as simple as you can. Your options are to either buy, don't buy, or redo your budget (and then ultimately buy). When you're faced with the decision to buy something, four simple questions should be able to point you in the right direction.

Did you budget for it? If yes, then buy it. If no, then can you afford it by using your discretionary budget? If yes, then buy it. If no, then is it a need or a want? If it's a need, you should have budgeting for it, in which case, redo your budget. If it's a want, then decide if you are willing to redo your budget to include it. Here's a flow chart you can use to help you make those decisions and keep your budget intact.

Figure 7.1

Now you're making significant changes and moving closer to financial freedom. Implementing the strategies and mindset described in this chapter represent another turning point in your script. You are moving through the second act. Opening new accounts, automating the allocation of your income toward your goals, and establishing Ulysses agreements to protect yourself from yourself all push you past the point of no return. Your commitment to these techniques will eliminate your ability to turn back.

Living within your means is the first step in accomplishing other goals. The money uncovered in your budget and made available through maintaining your balance can be used to pay off debt, save for the future, or some combination of both. In the next chapter we look at strategies specifically designed to help you achieve those goals.

Chapter Notes

1) *Catch Me If You Can*, DreamWorks, 2002

2) *Your Money or Your Life*, Vicki Robin, Penguin Books, 2008

3) *Richest Man in Babylon*, George S. Clason, Berkeley, Revised edition, 2002 (original 1926)

4) "Getting off the hedonic treadmill, one step at a time: The impact of regular religious practice and exercise on well-being"; Daniel Mochon, Michael I. Norton, *Journal of Economic Psychology*, Nov. 2008

8: Catching Up and Getting Ahead

"What can be added to the happiness of a man who is in health, out of debt, and has a clear conscience?"
—Adam Smith, the father of modern economics

Now that you have created a margin between your income and your expenses and implemented strategies to maintain that balance, it's time to start achieving your other goals. While you can certainly work on multiple goals simultaneously, there is an order you should follow in addressing and managing them.

Much like the need to master living within your means before moving on to this next step, if you carry any debt, it's important to pay it down before trying to focus too much effort on getting ahead. That doesn't mean you need to be completely debt free before you start building your savings. But you should put a priority on eliminating credit cards and consumer loans first. Mortgages, student debt, auto loans or anything with a fixed interest rate and payment schedule can be managed alongside your savings goals.

Whether you're interested in paying off debt to catch up or build your savings to get ahead, this chapter is meant to help guide you in the right direction. The strategies discussed are not one-size-fits-all and everyone has unique circumstances that deserve thoughtful consideration.

There can be serious and long-lasting consequences for not applying the correct solution for your situation and there are experts who can help you. This chapter is meant only to help you get started on your journey.

Eliminating the burden of debt

In Chapter 5 we discussed how debt inflates our perceived spending power and enables us to live beyond our means. Credit allows us to consume more than we otherwise should, and we end up unnecessarily spending our resources on the cost of interest. Debt is the biggest waste of your money and the largest threat to your ability to sustainably live below your means. This waste of money, especially when it could have been used to provide any one of your lifestyle needs, is contributing to your financial stress.

If you are trying to achieve financial freedom, make the most of your income, and accomplish your goals, you need to eliminate the burden of debt. Paying off debt and no longer relying on credit provides a reset so you can get back to managing your finances within your true means.

A quick note on mortgages: It is important to consider that they are not like other debts. You're essentially renting money from the bank, which you then use to own a place to live. The alternative would be to rent a home, fulfilling your need for shelter, but leaving you with nothing to show for it when you no longer live there.

Renting a home can go on forever. But renting money from a bank with a schedule for repayment means your "rent" payments will end when your loan is repaid and you're no longer renting money from the bank. For this reason, when eliminating debt, I encourage people not to consider a mortgage as a part of their debt, with a couple of exceptions:

- If your home is not a primary residence or if it is an investment property, then you can't really use the argument of paying rent as an alternative to owning.

Mortgages used to buy vacation homes or rental properties should be included in your debt calculations.

- If you keep refinancing or taking equity out of the home, then you are no longer paying it off. Instead, you're perpetually renting money from the bank and it's no different than being a renter with regards to how long it can continue. If you use your house as a piggy bank, then any second mortgages or equity lines should be considered debt.

- If the value of your home isn't growing or goes down at a rate faster than your payments can reduce your mortgage balance, then you are "upside down." The difference between the market value of your home and the amount you owe should be looked at as debt.

- If your goal is to pay off your mortgage.

If any of these scenarios apply to your situation, then add these amounts to your list of debt before deciding on your payoff strategy.

Start with a clear picture

To start eliminating your debt, you need a clear picture of exactly where you stand. List all your loans including the interest rate, total balance, minimum payment, and number of payments remaining for each. See the following table for an example that includes two credit cards, an auto loan, and a personal line of credit. This will help to better understand multiple liabilities.

Issuer	Rate	Balance	Minimum Payment	Payments Remaining
Auto Loan	4.5%	$ 12,000	$ 360	36 months
Personal Loan	8%	$ 14,000	$ 300	56 months
Credit Card 1	12%	$ 7,500	$ 150	248 months
Credit Card 2	14%	$ 8,500	$ 170	305 months

Figure 8.1

This information should be available from your account statements. While fixed loans with defined repayment terms have a set date when payments will end, revolving credit card debt can make it difficult to identify the number of payments remaining. Credit card statements generally highlight the number of months it would take to pay off the balance if you make only the minimum payments.

It is important to understand that making only the minimum payment is a very inefficient way to pay off a credit card because, as the balance is reduced the minimum payment is lowered. In the example above I assumed the greater of a $25 or 2% minimum payment.

The next piece of information you want to find is the *total cost of credit*. This is the total amount you will end up paying (both principal and interest) by the time you have paid off your debt.

Calculating the total payments on a fixed loan is fairly straight forward, simply multiply the payment amount by the number of payments remaining. The auto loan from the table above has a $360 payment and 36 months of payments remaining, $360 x 36 = $12,960. If you subtract the outstanding balance of the loan from that figure you would identify the total amount of interest you will end up paying over the remaining life of that loan, $12,960 - $12,000 = $960 in interest charges.

Credit cards, however, are not as easy to calculate because of the changes to the minimum payment as your outstanding balance decreases. If this figure is not provided on your credit card statement, you will likely need to use an online calculator to find the answer. You can search for a "credit card minimum payment calculator" or use websites like Bankrate.com or Creditcards.com to find the total cost to pay off your credit cards if only the minimum payments are made.

Issuer	Rate	Balance	Minimum Payment	Payments Remaining	Total Cost of Credit
Auto Loan	4.5%	$ 12,000	$ 360	36 months	$12,960
Personal Loan	8%	$ 14,000	$ 300	56 months	$16,800
Credit Card 1	12%	$ 7,500	$ 150	248 months	$14,240
Credit Card 2	14%	$ 8,500	$ 170	305 months	$19,285

Figure 8.2

When you list all your debt you can begin to see the big picture. Total up the balance, minimum payment, and cost of credit columns to see exactly how much you owe, your total monthly payments, and how much it would cost to pay off your debt if you make only the minimum payments.

The payments remaining column does not need to be totaled up because your payments are happening simultaneously, however make note of the debt with the longest time to payoff as this would be the length of time it would take to be debt free at the minimum payment pace.

The "Rate" column can be a little tricky to tally up. You will want to calculate a *weighted average* since different balances will impact the weight of each corresponding interest rate. Finding the weighted average will allow you to better understand how much you are spending every year on interest relative to the total balance that you owe. This calculation will also be helpful if you are considering refinancing your debt which I will cover later in this chapter.

The easiest way to calculate the weighted average is to multiply each balance by the corresponding interest rate to find an approximate annual finance charges or interest that will be paid for each loan. As an example, the auto loan in the above table has an interest rate of 4.5%. Multiply the balance of $12,000 by 0.045 to find the annual finance charge ($12,000 x 0.045 = $540). Although I did not include this in the following table you can also divide that by 12 to see the monthly finance charge. Do this for each debt and add them together to find the total annual finance charges.

Divide the Annual Finance Charges by the Balance to find the weighted average interest rate. ($3,750 ÷ $42,000 = 8.93%)

Issuer	Rate	Balance	Annual Finance Charges
Auto Loan	4.5%	$12,000	$ 540
Credit Card 1	12%	$ 7,500	$ 900
Credit Card 2	14%	$ 8,500	$ 1,190
Personal Loan	8%	$ 14,000	$ 1,120
Weighted Avg. / Totals	**8.93%**	$42,000	$3,750

Figure 8.3

After calculating the weighted average interest rate you will have completed totaling up your debt table. You can now clearly see the big picture.

Issuer	Rate	Balance	Minimum Payment	Payments Remaining	Total Cost of Credit
Auto Loan	4.5%	$ 12,000	$ 360	36 months	$12,960
Personal Loan	8%	$ 14,000	$ 300	56 months	$16,800
Credit Card 1	12%	$ 7,500	$ 150	248 months	$14,240
Credit Card 2	14%	$ 8,500	$ 170	305 months	$19,285
Totals	8.93%	$42,000	$980	305 months*	$63,285

*Number of months until all debt is paid making only minimum payments.

Figure 8.4

Looking at the total balance and minimum payments can be a little overwhelming. Debt doesn't typically develop overnight, and it probably won't get paid off overnight either. Your commitment to changing your ways will be tested through this process, so let's take a minute to dive into the numbers and really make the case for why it's so important to pay off your debt.

In the example from the previous chart, $980 a month is being allocated toward minimum debt payments. Comparing your total minimum monthly debt payments to your monthly income can help you to see exactly how much is being committed to debt repayment. You may already be aware of your debt-to-income ratio, but think back to the relativity heuristic and the question of what your time is worth. Consider how many hours a month you need to work just to cover your debt payments. What else would you rather use that time and effort for?

Distinguishing between principal and interest can be a powerful eye-opener. Understanding how much you are paying each year in interest can help you see how much of your resources are being wasted. The interest payments slow down your ability to pay back your debt and prevent you from allocating your money toward more important goals.

Imagine if you didn't have to pay interest and 100 percent of your payments were going toward principal. Simply dividing your balance by the monthly payment would show you the number of months it would take to completely settle your debt. Say you owe $10,000 at no interest and your monthly payment was $250, your debt would be paid off in 40 months. But say you owe $10,000 at 10 percent interest, it would take an additional 9 months or approximately $2,200 to pay off that same debt.

Looking at how much more you could pay off if you were not held back by interest payments on your debt highlights an obvious comparison to savings potential. If you didn't have any debt and instead were able to allocate your minimum monthly payments toward savings, you could essentially build savings equal to your current debt in as many months. Using the rule of 72 discussed in Chapter 4, consider what that could be worth in 10, 20 or even 30 years.

Highlighting this opportunity cost is not intended to make you feel guilty for using debt, but it may help you recognize how it is preventing you from accomplishing your goals and motivate you to embrace an alternative use of your resources.

Choosing how much to pay

The budgeting process allowed you to set and prioritize your goals. However, recognizing *what* you want to accomplish is only part of the equation. You can't solve the puzzle without knowing *when* you want to accomplish your goals. Obviously, the more you have allocated toward your goals, the greater they can be or the quicker you can achieve them.

When it comes to paying off debt, you have a couple of options. You can set a target date for when you want to be debt-free and solve for how much it would take per month to make that happen. Or you can identify the amount of money available for paying off debt through the budgeting process and calculate the time it will take at that rate. Either way, you control the time frame by the amount of money you are allotting toward your goal.

My recommendation is to use the budgeting process to identify the surplus amount you can afford to allocate toward your goal and accept the time frame corresponding to that amount. That's not to say you can't have a time frame in mind that plays into your priorities and compromises you determined during your budgeting process. Perhaps you want to be debt-free by a certain age, or prior to a major life event like marriage or retirement. Keep in mind that putting too much emphasis on timing may encourage you to create a goal that is too aggressive or not realistic.

Payoff strategies

The interest you pay on your debt slows down your ability to pay back the money you've borrowed. Loans with fixed terms will gradually apportion more of your payment toward principal as payments are made. The amortization of your payment schedule means that the opportunity to pay the principal balance is only available after first satisfying the interest portion of your payment. Paying off debt becomes particularly difficult when your available resources barely cover the interest-laden minimum payments.

Paying off your debt will require you to overcome the interest hurdle by paying more toward principal after fulfilling the interest burden. Then, as the principal balance of your debt becomes smaller and the interest hurdle is lowered, you will pay down more principal.

Starting from this moment—if you don't borrow any more—the minimum payment you must make on credit cards will gradually be lowered as your balance is paid down. If you simply maintained the current payment level, even though the minimum payment required is decreasing, you can essentially "overpay" and accelerate the payoff.

Snowball method

If you have multiple debts, and while paying more than your minimum payments you are able to pay off one of them, maintaining your payment level and applying even more to your other debts will further accelerate your payoff timeline. This snowball effect, named after the way a snowball grows as it rolls through snow, is a positive feedback loop that enables you to gather payoff momentum as more debt is settled. Applying some strategy to how much you overpay, and which debts you allocate those overpayments to, can dramatically reduce the time and cost of paying off your debt.

Take another look at the example of debts listed previously:

Issuer	Rate	Balance	Minimum Payment
Auto Loan	4.5%	$ 12,000	$ 360
Personal Loan	8%	$ 14,000	$ 300
Credit Card 1	12%	$ 7,500	$ 150
Credit Card 2	14%	$ 8,500	$ 170
Weighted Avg. / Totals	**8.93%**	$ 42,000	$ 980

Figure 8.5

For this example, let's assume that after budgeting we uncovered $400 to allocate toward our goal of paying off debt. The first strategy to consider is the momentum-building snowball method. This method pays the minimum payments on all debt and applies the extra payment amount to the debt with the lowest balance regardless of interest rate. Then once that debt is paid off, you can add the payment amount that had been applied to the first debt to the extra payment amount of the second debt by order of balance.

Payoff Order	Issuer	Rate	Balance	Monthly Payment
1	Credit Card 1	12%	$ 7,500	$ 150 + $ 400
2	Credit Card 2	14%	$ 8,500	$ 170
3	Auto Loan	4.5%	$ 12,000	$ 360
4	Personal Loan	8%	$ 14,000	$ 300

Figure 8.6

With this strategy, Credit Card 1 with a balance of $7,500 would get the full $400 overpayment. Additional payments will reduce the minimum payment the credit card company charges. However, if you maintain your payment at $550 ($150, plus the extra $400), this credit card should be paid off in approximately 15 months.

After satisfying Credit Card 1, the previous total payment amount of $550 is then applied to the next largest balance on the list—in this example, Credit Card 2. The approximate remaining balances and monthly payment would look something like this:

Payoff Order	Issuer	Rate	Balance	Monthly Payment
~~1~~	~~Credit Card 1~~	~~12%~~	$ 0	$ 0
2	Credit Card 2	14%	$ 7,100	$ 170 + $ 550
3	Auto Loan	4.5%	$ 7,500	$ 360
4	Personal Loan	8%	$ 11,000	$ 300

Figure 8.7

Remember, even though your monthly minimums on some of your debts are going down each month, keep paying the original monthly minimum that you have budgeted for.

The snowball effect now adds the payment that was being made on Credit Card 1 to the Credit Card 2 minimum payment when this accelerated payoff strategy began, or $720 per month! The balance of Credit Card 2 should be paid off in approximately 11 months. After Credit Card 2 is paid off, the $720 monthly amount that was paid on this debt will be applied to the auto loan. The following chart shows the approximate remaining balances and payments at that point.

Payoff Order	Issuer	Rate	Balance	Monthly Payment
~~1~~	~~Credit Card 1~~	~~12%~~	$ 0	$ 0
~~2~~	~~Credit Card 2~~	~~14%~~	$ 0	$ 0
3	Auto Loan	4.5%	$4,200	$ 360 + $ 720
4	Personal Loan	8%	$ 8,700	$ 300

Figure 8.8

In this example, after 26 months, both credit cards have been paid off and $1,080 per month is being applied to the Auto Loan. The payoff momentum has radically picked up speed and will have the Auto Loan satisfied in just four months!

Payoff Order	Issuer	Rate	Balance	Monthly Payment
~~1~~	~~Credit Card 1~~	~~12%~~	$ 0	$ 0
~~2~~	~~Credit Card 2~~	~~14%~~	$ 0	$ 0
~~3~~	~~Auto Loan~~	~~4.5%~~	$ 0	$ 0
4	Personal Loan	8%	$ 7,700	$ 300 + $1,080

Figure 8.9

Finally, the full force of the snowball effect — all $1,380 per month — will be applied to the remaining Personal Loan. The balance of approximately $7,150 will be completely paid off in six months.

In our example, the entire debt balance—$42,000—was satisfied in three years by paying an additional $400 and committing to maintaining the beginning minimum payments throughout the payoff strategy.

The snowball method is not always the quickest, or even the cheapest strategy. The benefit of this approach is the psychological motivation that comes from paying off debt and making progress toward your goal.

Avalanche method

An alternative to the snowball method is the avalanche method, which attacks the highest interest rates regardless of balance. Since the drag of interest on your debt is ultimately what holds you back from paying off your debt, the higher the interest rate, the greater the barrier. By attacking the highest interest rate first, you mitigate interest expense and the drag it has on your payoff plan.

The fundamentals of this process are almost exactly the same as the snowball method we covered step by step. The only difference is that you would organize your debts by interest rate rather than balance.

What's the best payoff strategy?

Paying off debt is a big undertaking. At the heart of the issue is the desire to eliminate wasting your resources on debt interest payments. You must overcome the hurdle of interest before any of your payment can go toward paying down the amount you owe. Limiting the money wasted on interest would seem to be the most practical and least expensive way of paying off your debt. However, the best strategy may be more than just the quickest or least expensive approach.

A Harvard Business Review article summarized a research project designed to study this question. The article is titled "Repayment Concentration and Consumer Motivation to Get Out of Debt."[1] Along with three colleagues, Boston College Questrom School of Business Associate Professor Remi Trudel did a field study of indebted consumers with multiple debt accounts.

Through several experiments, they determined that people feel better about their efforts based on the amount paid off relative to any one balance rather than the overall amount of repayment or how much debt is left to be paid.

Say you had $10,000 in debt made up of a $2,000 car loan and a $8,000 credit card. If $1,000 could be applied to these debts, you would likely feel more motivated if half of the car loan was paid down rather than one-eighth of the credit card regardless of the interest rates or minimum payments of those debts.

The researchers found that small wins provided the greatest sense of progress and in turn provided a feeling of motivation. Given the difficulty of changing your spending habits and paying off your debt, you may find that this motivation can help you to stick with your payoff plan.

Without these small wins, the temptation to slow down or even suspend your payoff effort may derail you from achieving your goal altogether. This would suggest that the snowball method, starting with the smallest balance first, is the method most likely to lead toward success.

There is no right or wrong answer; there is simply what works best for you. In addition to using online calculators to better understand interest, minimum payments, and the time it will take to pay off debt, unbury.me is a great website that can help you decide which method to use and understand the time and cost differences between them.

Reduce what you pay by moving balances to your own lower-rate card or take a zero-percent offer

No doubt you've seen offers to open a new credit card and transfer your balance. Applying effort to limiting or lowering the interest you pay may be a good strategy to consider.

This can be a viable option if you can trade an 18% interest rate for 0% interest. However, beware of the risks. Usually these offers institute a much-higher rate should you miss a payment. Also, to prevent "card hopping," the new card agreement might contain fine print stating that you must keep the card active for a certain number of months. If not, you'll probably have to pay interest retroactive to the date you first transferred the balance.

If you already have multiple cards, you may not want to open a new card. Instead, you might want to consider moving balances within your own card inventory, if there is room on a card with a lower interest rate. Remember the math from the snowball method that helped you figure out the effective interest rate or the weighted average interest rate. If moving balances between cards can dramatically impact the weighted average interest rate you're paying on your debt, why not? At the same time you move a balance to a lower-rate card, **CLOSE** the higher-rate account and never use it again.

Debt refinance or consolidation

While debt refinancing or consolidation is an option for some, if you haven't learned to change your behavior and prioritize, you can go right back to overspending. If the reason you are in the hole is spending on things you don't need, what will stop you from returning to the same habit of overspending and using debt?

Start with debt payoff strategies first. In general, once you've got at least half your debt paid off, you're demonstrating that you've built a new system to deal with your spending and are sticking to it. Only then should you consider if some type of debt consolidation or refinance plan could be more efficient for you. It could even be beneficial to swap revolving debt for debt tied to an asset, like your home.

Consider the weighted average interest rate, total minimum payments, and total cost of credit you calculated earlier in this chapter to decide if refinancing or consolidating your debt will make a significant enough improvement. If you feel this might work for you, consult a professional to help you understand all the pros and cons of going this route.

When your debt seems insurmountable

Sometimes past decisions and circumstances can knock your finances way out of balance. Your accumulated debt may have grown beyond your ability to pay it off. Or maybe you've experienced a significant change in income preventing you from making even minimum payments, let alone overpayments to reduce your balance. If this is your situation, you may have to step up to more last-resort solutions to deal with your debt.

One possibility is to use funds from your own assets. This can include borrowing against 401(k) savings or getting a home equity loan. These loans usually come at low interest rates, much cheaper than credit cards. In the case of 401(k) loans, you pay yourself back, not a bank, with all interest on the loan going right back into your 401(k) account.

If those options will not work for you, then you may need to seek qualified professionals who can guide you through credit counseling, renegotiation, or even bankruptcy. Professional help will result in additional costs, so don't enter into these options lightly. However, a reset may be your way back to finding a balance in your personal finances.

Bankruptcy

Yes, even bankruptcy. Just the word has connotations of failure. But the remedy is there for a reason and is a strategy that can provide you with a fresh start. As pointed out previously in this book, it's time to tackle the problem, not indulge in self-shaming over your situation.

Bankruptcy is a federal legal process with two options that are most commonly used by individuals:

- Chapter 7 liquidation, where you sell property to pay creditors.
- Chapter 13, where you create a three- to five-year payment plan to repay at least a portion of your debt to creditors.

Both types of bankruptcy work toward a "discharge" order from the court that prevents creditors from continuing collection efforts. Some types of debt aren't included, but the discharge alone can protect you from creditors, relieve stress, and provide you with a plan for getting your finances back under control.

Please note that this information on debt consolidation, refinancing, renegotiation, loans from personal assets, and bankruptcy is not a recommendation or financial advice. I've included it just to make you aware of options for dealing with your debt. Again, seek advice from qualified professionals if you want to explore any of these options further.

Stay on track, and reward yourself too: The 75/25 Rule

Priorities and desires may change over time. After establishing your payoff plan, you could lose motivation or be discouraged when all your extra cash is going to pay off debt. You may start to make concessions or maybe something comes up that throws you off your spending plan. Like losing weight, you're working out, eating right for a while, but then that weekend comes when you splurge. It's hard to get back to the discipline of your new routine.

The 75/25 rule can help you overcome this challenge.

If we've identified the same $400 surplus as before, rather than use all of it to pay down debt, put 75 percent or $300 toward debt and the other 25 percent or $100 into a savings account. It will take a bit longer to pay down your debt, but in six months you'll have built up savings of $600, or $1,200 in a year's time.

Then, if an unexpected expense comes up, rather than taking you out of your rhythm in paying down your debt, you have money set aside. You'll have a cushion in reserve for something like a car repair, or even an opportunity to enjoy a once-in-a-lifetime opportunity like a concert or other event. Now that expense won't go back on a credit card and won't sabotage your debt payment plan.

If you continue putting aside the 25 percent, and don't spend it, then that savings is going to continue to grow and grow. At a certain point, you don't need to build it larger. Say you've been working the plan and your savings account balance reaches $1,500. Take some or all of it and retire a big chunk of your debt with one "power payment." It's great motivation and will give you the emotional reward of feeling like you're ahead of the game.

This safety element of saving 25 percent prevents you from "falling off the wagon" and provides satisfaction when you can take big steps forward toward your goals.

The savings account you build using the 75/25 rule can, in effect, replace your need to use a credit card. I call it an "inverse credit card" because you build up a balance to draw from, rather than drawing down a balance that you must pay back with interest. After a "charge" to the account, then you pay yourself to rebuild the balance with no finance charges (and even a bit of interest earned).

It's another protection against throwing your plan off track.

Getting ahead

Financial freedom occurs when your income is enough to provide for the things that you need, when you are no longer held back by the stress of not having enough, and when it's possible to get ahead.

While maintaining your balance and living within your means is a significant achievement, if all you do is learn to live within the limits of your income, you are always dependent on your income.

At the end of the day, your income is subject to change and your ability to earn a living is susceptible to risk. Your income potential may ultimately be limited by your ability or desire to do the things you need to do to earn your income. At some point you might not want to keep going to the same job day in and day out. Or, you may not be able—or willing—to continue earning your present income.

Getting ahead is about building a cushion that either protects you from an interruption in income or provides you with options to change where and how you earn what you need. Beyond a cushion, these savings can be used for large purchases outside your established budget.

Building savings

Living within your means, paying off debt, and no longer relying on debt to maintain your lifestyle, will inevitably leave you with some amount of money at the end of every month. Whether you are building general wealth, or saving for retirement, a large future purchase, or even a little extra for a vacation (remember the pay-in-advance mindset we discussed in Chapter 4), setting aside this extra money sets you on a path toward your savings goals.

Unlike the debt payoff strategies we discussed earlier, savings goals can and should be tackled simultaneously. Use a compartmentalization strategy to break up your saving goals into groups based on the time it takes to achieve them, or when you need them to be achieved. The simplest categories to use are short-term, intermediate-term, and long-term savings.

You may want to further categorize your savings goals within these time frames based on importance and dollar amount. This will help you to prioritize your savings goals, and if you need to make changes to your savings efforts, you can quickly identify the goals that you need to adjust.

Short-term savings are generally amounts that take less than a couple of months to save or represent expenses that will take place soon.

Emergency savings and larger expenses outside your normal monthly budget are examples of things you want to cover with your short-term savings. Combining the inverse credit card strategy and 75/25 rule is a great way to establish and maintain short-term savings that frees you from debt.

Think about what you've been spending in addition to your monthly discretionary budget: Home maintenance, holidays and birthdays, back-to-school expenses, youth sports, and other spending that is predictable, but not part of a monthly budget.

Once your inverse credit card is funded, continue using the 75/25 rule to further build savings.

Next should be emergency savings. Remember the annual economic report that stated only 41 percent of households could cover a $400 emergency expense? Don't be part of that 41 percent! Start with an amount equal to one month of living expenses, then work up to somewhere between three to six months. These savings should also be set up in a short-term account that is liquid and accessible. Continue to protect your future-self by "insulating" this money with either no debit card or partitioning it into a separate savings account that you must transfer to your primary savings for access.

With emergency funds put away, it's time to start thinking about intermediate and long-term savings goals. These goals can be either necessary or discretionary, and depending on the size and priority you place on achieving them, can vary in length of time to fulfill. The budgeting process in Chapter 6 allows you to clearly identify these goals and establish a savings plan that fits within your monthly budget.

Much like deciding how much to pay toward your debt, you need to set savings goals based on what you have available and at least a target date for reaching those goals. You'll need to choose whether to prioritize your lifestyle or your goals of saving toward the future.

Intermediate-term goals can range in dollar amount and time to achieve. Generally they are larger expenses like vacations, a new car, or even a down payment for a house. The idea is that you can achieve these goals in one to five years.

Long-term goals usually represent a significant dollar amount and, because of their size, can take more than five years to achieve. The most common include retirement, college savings, or just general wealth. These long-term savings goals are sensitive to taxes and market risk, and sometimes have restrictions and contribution limits. Planning for these long-term goals is a discipline in itself, and for most people, is a part of a financial plan where you should seek professional advice.

These long-term goals are not easy to achieve, but the sooner you start the better off you'll be. Depending on when you start this journey and how much time you give yourself to achieve your goals, there is a chance that some of these long-term goals need to be aggressively pursued in an intermediate-term time frame.

Take retirement as an example. You have only a couple of choices when you reach your target retirement age and don't have the savings you're going to need. You can either accept not having enough and learn to live on less or work longer.

Rather than simply accept those two options, the earlier you address these goals, the more you can control the outcome. The third option, of course, is to set aside savings between now and the date you want to achieve your goal, but that option needs time.

It takes a long time to pay off debt and build up savings. Regardless of where you start or where you would like to be, you have the tools to achieve your goals. Establishing a plan to get you there is the first and, quite frankly, the hardest step.

Because these are long-term goals, the next important step in achieving financial freedom is the mindset and the motivation to stick with your plan no matter what obstacles come your way.

You've come a long way already. In the next chapter you will review what it takes to continue down this path toward financial freedom and where you can find the encouragement and support to keep going.

Chapter Notes

1) "Repayment Concentration and Consumer Motivation to Get Out of Debt"; Remi Trudel, Keri L. Kettle, Simon J. Blanchard, Gerald Häubl; *Journal of Consumer Research*; Vol. 43, Issue 3, October 2016

9: The Balancing Act

"They always say that time changes things,
but you actually have to change
them yourself."
—Andy Warhol

It will take time for your financial situation to change, but it's not changing because of time. If anything, letting time go by without actively addressing your situation will likely make things worse, or at least not as good as they could be. Remember the Rule of 72? When it comes to building wealth, time can be a powerful multiplier. It can also be a major obstacle.

By understanding the financial challenges you face and implementing the processes laid out in this book, you'll be making the changes necessary to achieve your goals. Time is just a part of the equation.

Your commitment to the changes you're making will be tested. You will be tempted to spend more or save less, to slow down your progress or change your priorities altogether. You will have to stick with your plan to achieve your goals and time will test your resolve.

It's also inevitable that you'll need to make changes to your plan. Circumstances outside your control will come along, and you will have to decide if they are merely temptations or legitimate needs for change. How you handle these situations will be a big factor in determining your success.

Wash, rinse, repeat – the shampoo algorithm

You probably recognize this or a similar phrase from the directions on practically every bottle of shampoo. In computer programming it is jokingly referred to as an endless loop. Earlier in the book we highlighted some of the ways marketers manipulate our buying behavior, so I wouldn't put it past any of those folks to encourage unnecessary overuse of their products just to get us to buy more.

Joking aside, managing your financial balance should be an endless loop. The average shampoo-user probably knows how many times to wash his or her hair. But average people probably don't know how many times—or how frequently—they need to reevaluate their budgets, track their spending, or reassess their needs, wants, priorities, and goals. This is not a one-and-done exercise.

Not all reasons for reevaluation are negative. Some will be overwhelmingly positive. Pay raises, bonuses, promotions, even the reduction of debt or the slow steady appreciation of money you've set aside can give you reason to change your spending and saving behavior. Your response to positive changes will test your commitment. Remember the concept of adaptation; if you are not disciplined in your budgeting and lifestyle choices, you could end up living right up to the limit of your means. And if you're not careful, exceeding them once again.

This doesn't mean that you need to deprive yourself of any enjoyment that comes with an increase to your income. It is reasonable to improve your standard of living as your income improves.

It simply means you should be regularly reevaluating your necessary and discretionary expenses, along with your goals. Prioritize your needs, wants, and goals so that you can account for and provide the things that are important to you both right now and in the future.

As goals and priorities change, or you find that you are ahead of or behind schedule, you may need to make adjustments. There are only a few variables you can adjust: the dollar amount, the achievement date, and the actions you take between now and that desired achievement date. Reevaluating your goals on a regular basis gives you an opportunity to make adjustments to stay on track, so you can achieve your goals within the timeframe you've set.

You may need to go back into parts of this book multiple times to revisit concepts or processes that helped you on your path toward financial freedom. Unlike shampoo, this book doesn't run out. So, read, implement, and repeat as much and as often as you like.

Contentment – a frame of mind

By establishing a lifestyle that fits within your means and maintaining a budget that accounts for your goals, you are taking control of your path toward financial freedom. Living comfortably within your means eliminates the stress that comes from not having enough for what you need. By prioritizing your needs and wants, you are focusing on what is most important to you. You actively create your own personalized hierarchy of needs that applies your resources in the order that you want. You prevent yourself from wasting money on things that don't matter or carry little importance for your life.

A lifestyle that provides the needs that you find most important, as well as a path to achieving your financial goals, is likely to produce a feeling of satisfaction. This contentment with what you have can suppress your desire for more, prevent you from living beyond your means, and help you escape the rat race of chasing additional income.

Whether by lowering the bar or making more, achieving financial freedom—maintaining a balance between what you need and what you have—is about having more than enough. If you never define how much "enough" is, how can you know when you attain it? If the only limiting factor to your spending is how much you make, then even when you have extra it will never register as more than enough.

Creating a balance between what you need and what you have is as much about defining when you feel satisfied as it is about how much you have or have access to. When you control your desire for more, then you eliminate the need for credit cards and basic consumer debt. Granted, large purchases like a car, a house, or a college education may still require some leverage, but you are free from dependence on borrowed money.

The frame of mind that you have enough, or that you don't need more, is not a mental state that is easy to achieve or sustain. Even after fulfilling your needs and finding contentment, you may be tempted by outside influences to want more. Contentment is a rational thought. When all your needs are met, why would you want more? But as we have learned, we usually don't act rationally.

What are you going to do with that $1 million?

A good friend of mine shared a story with me that I think embodies rational behavior from someone who literally wrote the book about it.

On the day that Richard Thaler (cited previously and a major part of the inspiration for this book) was awarded the Nobel Prize in economics, my friend Sean happened to be touring the University of Chicago with his daughter. The school was buzzing with excitement over the fact that the economics department now had a Nobel Laureate among its faculty. There was so much buzz, in fact, that the itinerary for my friend's tour had to be changed given the attention that was drawn to the campus on this day.

Winning a Nobel Prize is clearly a big deal and recognition for a life's work in your field is probably very rewarding in itself. But the award also comes with the added benefit of a monetary award just shy of $1 million.

Following the tour, Sean and his daughter found a small fast food restaurant for lunch called Noodles Etc. And who else was there enjoying a cheap lunch? The very same Dr. Thaler.

Talk about walking the walk. How much more rational could you be? On the day of his Nobel Prize award, and soon to receive that million-dollar payout, his behavior was consistent with all that he preaches. He didn't justify why he should splurge on an expensive meal or take on a new, upscale persona. He acted rationally, content with his life and maintaining a long-term outlook.

Sometime later, as a guest on the "Freakonomics Radio" podcast[1], he was asked by host Stephen Dubner about the award. Thaler responded that "What are you going to do with the money?" seems to be the most frequently asked question of Nobel Prize winners. But to him—a behavioral economist—it's a silly question.

Dubner guessed why: "Because the answer would be, 'It just goes into the pool with the other money. It's no different than any other.' Is that why?"

"Right," responded Thaler. "The proceeds of that money, half of which will end up in the U.S. Treasury, are sitting in some account at Vanguard. And if I go out for a fancy dinner, there's no way for me to label that 'Nobel money.'"

He went on to muse that the hedonic thing to do would be to open a special account with a "Nobel Credit Card" that he could then use for "ridiculous" purchases.

But knowing what he knows, he'd prefer to stick with his Noodles Etc. lifestyle. As his research has shown, adaptation can lead us into a higher—and higher spending—lifestyle if we let it. Yet we will find no greater satisfaction or contentment chasing more and more.

Thaler's real-life behavior is a great example of how you can think differently with the new knowledge you've gained from this book:

- Know what money you truly have access to. (Note that Thaler immediately lopped taxes off his award.)
- Keep your goals in mind so you stay in control and achieve what's important to you.
- Build a long-term mindset, not one based on fleeting, short-term highs from spending.
- Use windfalls to accelerate your plan, not derail it.
- Seek everyday contentment, not a life of chasing more, bigger, and better.

Though we hope we can recognize what Thaler calls "silly" behavior in ourselves, some may find that a third party can be a great way to help you stay on track.

Accountability partners

Just as some people prefer to partner up with another person to go to the gym, financial accountability partners can be an effective way for people to stay on track. When you partner with a person, or group of people, you've committed to each other that you have not been managing your finances efficiently and need to change. Your partners keep you motivated and can provide a regular check on your progress.

Who are your potential accountability partners?

It could be your spouse. If you are going through this together, there should naturally be mutual support for building and adhering to a budget and working toward your goals. Clearly, if stress over money has created stress in your relationship, working toward greater harmony is an excellent motivator to keep each other on track.

On the other hand, working with a spouse could be a *source* of stress when one of you needs to call the other out for straying from the plan. You also both have the same emotional influences that could work against you. For example, kids pushing back against lifestyle changes or still wanting to "keep up" with their peer group.

An alternative to your spouse could be to choose a third party, such as a friend, as your partner. Also, some community colleges, adult schools, churches, and other organizations offer financial stewardship courses. You and fellow class members could stick together beyond the course to form an accountability group.

One stipulation for third-party partners is that all are willing to share completely about their financial situations and keep what is shared within the confines of the group. Without agreement to be honest and keep information confidential, the effectiveness of this type of partner can be diminished. Another thing to consider is that a third-party relationship, whether it's a friend or group member, could change. If that happens, will they maintain their confidentiality?

Should I use a financial professional as a partner?

For a financial professional to be a valuable accountability partner, they need to be more than just an asset manager. Investment selection, products, or even cost and performance are not always significant differentiators. Account types and investment vehicles are important parts of strategically managing your wealth. But, with so many similar offerings, financial services have become commoditized.

To find a professional who also can be a good accountability partner, be sure to ask them about the process they use to help their clients. Do they help you set a budget?

Do they help you set goals and build an overall plan? Do they talk in terms of living within your means and gaining financial freedom from overspending and debt? Positive answers to those questions will help you find the right fit.

Thinking back to Maslow's hierarchy, there is also a "security need" that can be satisfied by working with a financial professional. Worrying about sharing your financial details with a friend or group is a valid concern, but a professional has a duty to keep your details private and maintain a professional relationship.

Finally, an impartial third-party can be a good way to help you remove emotion from your decisions and keep your plan grounded in reality.

Your balancing act

We began this book comparing the typical screenplay plotline to your path toward achieving financial freedom. Here's the plotline again as a reminder.

Stage 1 Setup	Stage 2 New Situation	Stage 3 Progress	Stage 4 Complications	Stage 5 Final Push	Stage 6 Aftermath
Turning Point #1 Opportunity	Turning Point #2 Change of Plans	Turning Point #3 Point of no Return	Turning Point #4 Major Setback	Turning Point #5 Climax	
Act 1		Act 2		Act 3	

Figure 1.1

At the beginning, you see the *Opportunity* to improve your financial situation, whether by getting out of debt, building your personal wealth, or simply learning to live comfortably within your means. Achieving these goals requires a *Change in Plans* around how you spend your money.

We explored why we act the way we do with our money, the psychology of fulfilling needs, and the way our minds can work against us in achieving our goals. We made *Progress* by learning how to overcome these challenges, set reasonable goals, and implement strategies to achieve them.

The budgeting process allowed you to see where you are now and how to get to where you want to be by prioritizing and compromising to allocate your resources toward what is important to you. The sacrifices you make in that process push you past the *Point of no Return*, though complications and challenges will continue to stand between you and your success.

There may be *Major Setbacks* that seem to prevent you from moving forward. In the movies, it's just a necessary part of the story that creates tension and makes the victory that much sweeter and propels the movie into the third and final act.

For you and your script, it doesn't need to be a big deal. These setbacks will come and go. You will stumble and you will get back up. Keep focusing on the long-term objectives and revisit your priorities, refine your goals, distinguish between your needs and wants, and just keep pushing toward success.

The *Final Push* in our script, and what stands between you and your ultimate goal of financial freedom, is action by you to stick to your plan and use the balance between what you need and what you have to either pay off debt, save for the future, or some combination of both.

The wash, rinse, and repeat approach will keep you moving in the right direction. Furthermore, using accountability partners can help you to stay on track even if major setbacks seem to derail your efforts.

If you can, then the *Aftermath* will be contentment and financial freedom.

My goal in writing this book was to help others overcome the struggles that I have seen so many experience—including myself. Since this was my first attempt at writing a book, I sought the wise counsel of other authors and writers much better at it than me. One bit of advice along this path that stood out was "if you want people to read it, keep it short."

So, if you found yourself glancing at the back of the book to see how many pages you were going to have to read, I've got good news for you. You can stop reading now and take away everything that I intended to impart. But I encourage you to keep reading. Let me share my personal story with you and a few stories from friends I have met along the way that add to the advice in this book.

My personal story

At some point while reading this book, you may have wondered what qualified me to understand the struggles that others may be going through with their finances. Thinking long-term and living within your means can be easier said than done and while I can't know the difficulty of overcoming every financial challenge, I have personally experienced setbacks of my own.

Early in my career, I was driven by earning money and enjoying the lifestyle it afforded. I sought the comfort of not just an income that exceeded my needs but the conveniences that came with it. I found satisfaction in not having to adhere to a budget or balance a checkbook. I constantly chased after an income that exceeded my lifestyle, and as my lifestyle improved to meet my income, it was immediately followed by an effort to raise my income again. I was stuck on the adaptation treadmill.

I have to say I'm a little embarrassed about that period of my life, my ego, and my focus on money. Looking back, I probably could have spent that money better.

But there are lessons learned and passing those along is now part of the work I do. The messages and advice in this book are not just abstract ideas. I understand the challenges and process of making radical adjustments to spending and lifestyle because I lived it.

Make more to live more

My drive for income led me to leave a career in the U.S. Navy after an eight-year enlistment. I left behind the security of a regular paycheck and the potential for a military pension in search of greener pastures and a job in financial services. In my mind, financial freedom was the product of making more money and all my life decisions at that point were about earning as much as possible.

I stumbled across a lucrative career as a sales rep for a mutual fund company. My ultimate goal was to be an outside sales rep, but as with most jobs, you have to work your way up to that. My career path started with a move to Kansas City, which, compared to the cost of living in San Diego, was a big boost to my lifestyle. I was single with no kids, in my 20s, making six figures, and well into the social belonging and esteem stages of Maslow's hierarchy.

One of the great benefits of my time in Kansas City and that stage in my life was that I met my wife. While we were dating, my spending shifted toward living a comfortable life, entertainment, travelling, going out to eat, and generally doing what we wanted, when we wanted and not thinking too much about it.

My lifestyle improves to meet my income

The year 2008 represented some very clear challenges for a lot of people, and while the economy was contracting and the stock market seemed to be falling uncontrollably, I found myself lucky enough to make it out unscathed. In 2009, with the confidence to provide for a family, my wife and I were married. Shortly after, I achieved my goal of landing an outside sales territory.

The promotion paid very well and just about doubled my income. But it was difficult. My sales territory was the entire East Coast. I'd leave on Monday morning and not return home until Friday. I was a road warrior, in a different city every day, and in a different hotel every night. Travel reward points and first-class upgrades from frequent flier status were my achievement badges. I remember running through a terminal to catch a connecting flight once, only to find that the plane had already pulled away from the gate by the time I got there. After the attendant asked who I was, she picked up her radio and asked the pilot to return to the gate so I could board. My ego relished in the benefits that money and status could provide.

But even though I was having success at chasing more income, I had very little to show for it because our lifestyle quickly grew to meet our means. We moved to St. Louis so my wife could be closer to family, as we wanted to start our own. We had a great house in an affluent neighborhood, I was driving a BMW, my wife was driving a Range Rover. We felt like we were on top of the world.

Another double in income

Another promotion doubled my income once again and it came with an executive-sounding title. But the work load and expectations were much more. Most of my income was commission-based and there was a direct correlation between how hard I worked and how much I got paid. The promotion came with a move to the San Francisco Bay Area, where housing costs were significantly higher than the Midwest. However, my territory was just Northern California and Oregon, so I was traveling much less.

Despite the higher income, our lifestyle continued to equal our means. Before the next payday, the money would flow out just as fast as it was coming in. I couldn't remember the last time I had created a budget, let alone balanced a checkbook. I thought financial freedom meant doing whatever I wanted whenever I wanted.

There was a five-year window during this time when a couple million dollars of income passed through my hands. It's embarrassing to think back to the amount of money I wasted on a lifestyle that did little to secure my long-term goals. Granted, half of that income went to the government in taxes, but the other half seemed to just evaporate into thin air.

Despite the income, debt lured me in

With all my "discretionary" income, I became more willing to take on credit card debt. I knew I could pay it off at any time so carrying a balance of $15,000 didn't seem like a bad idea. Then it became a slippery slope, and soon it was two credit cards, with $15,000 to $20,000 on each of them.

I was probably past the point where I could simply pay them off, but it didn't discourage me from spending because of the money that was flowing in every month. I justified my credit card debt because it seemed small relative to my income (relativity at its best). The amount of money I spent on interest just servicing those cards was ridiculous.

There was one purchase that stands out as a particularly poor use of credit. I decided to buy a new car and it was right after a great sales month when I received a big commission check. Even though I had enough money from that single paycheck to pay for the entire car, I only put a little money down and ended up financing the rest of it through the dealership because they offered a 0% interest rate.

I don't regret buying the car, but I do regret borrowing the money. It's funny to me that I talked myself into the purchase because of this large, outsized commission check, then avoided the pain of paying by borrowing the money. I can't for the life of me remember how I spent the rest of the money I "saved" from that commission check by taking out the loan.

An opportunity for change

A sense of anxiety started to nag me toward the end of 2015. Things were changing with my job, sales were down, the company was looking to cut costs and rumors were spreading about possible layoffs. Perhaps it was fear of the unthinkable, or maybe cognitive dissonance, but not wanting to believe it was possible to lose my job allowed me to keep my head down and work as hard as I could.

By April, however, the bomb hit. I got laid off.

It was a great job and I didn't lose it because I didn't do it well. The company just didn't need as many sales reps. There was a better way to structure their sales force, so they made the decision to let some of us go. These things happen.

Needless to say, I was not in a state of financial freedom. I was chasing after money and feeling the stress of not having enough. I was not in control of my spending and the lifestyle I had become accustomed to required a level of income that was not easy to maintain, let alone replace.

I was able to find another job quickly enough that still paid a good income. I wasn't starting at zero, but my wife and I had to reflect on what we truly needed and rework our budget to design a lifestyle that fit our new means. That required a lot of change.

That's why I see Maslow's hierarchy as a good model to understand the way I spend and the reason I spend. Of course I need the basics: a safe and secure place for my family to reside, food, water and shelter. Those were the priorities. Esteem needs—I didn't care anymore. There was no longer a desire to keep up with the Joneses because I admitted to the fact that I couldn't. Or, that I just didn't want to any more.

We reset our lifestyle and created a budget that covered our needs. Then, to the degree that our income exceeded that amount, we added the discretionary lifestyle expenses that we could afford. It was different than the lifestyle we had grown accustomed to, but the requirements were less and the burden of maintaining my previous income was lifted.

At the end of the day, having more than I needed was all that I was chasing.

The urge to make more money is logical. It seems like the easiest way to expand the balance between what we need and what we have. Yet, no matter how much I chased a higher paycheck, I could never really create a margin that way. Look back to the self-assessment question about your income increases in the past five years and see if that's true for you, too.

The lesson I learned is that the only real way to achieve that balance and contribute to that margin is to control and manage my spending.

Think more minimalist than hedonist

Another lesson learned was one of being a little bit more minimalist. I'm more conscious of what I'm really getting for my money. If it's not truly worth what I'm spending, then I don't do it.

No doubt it's a challenge to lower your standard of living —to lower your lifestyle. It seems impossible, but fight the "you only live once" or "fear of missing out" urge and think long-term instead.

This probably sounds trite, but I'm looking back at my significant change and I'm probably happier now making one quarter of what I used to. I'm still covering everything I need.

I still have a roof over my head, I provide for my family, and our expenses fall well within our means.

We prioritize what is important to us. When we go on vacation, we go where we can get the most bang for our buck. When we look at purchase options, we shop for utility rather than the latest and greatest model or brand name. We save toward spending goals rather than make spontaneous and hasty purchases. We no longer depend on borrowed money to satisfy our short-term desires. Instead, we focus on saving for long-term goals that will make things easier for my family in the future.

You don't have to make more. You need to spend less. It's doable and this book shows you how.

The title of the Freakonomics podcast featuring Richard Thaler referenced earlier in the chapter is "People Aren't Dumb. The World is Hard." It's a great message from a master at understanding our irrational financial behavior. We struggle with personal finances, not because we're not smart, but simply because we're human.

Up next is a reinforcement of that message. The next chapter is a collection of stories about people like you. I've included these stories for you to see how others have made changes to get closer to achieving the balance between what they need and what they have, and, ultimately, financial freedom. Read on for more lessons learned.

Chapter Notes

1) Freakonomics Radio Podcast, "People Aren't Dumb. The World is Hard.", July 11, 2018, Stephen J. Dubner, http://freakonomics.com/podcast/richard-thaler/

10: Personal Stories

*"And I found a whole group of friends who
have the same dream, and that makes us
sort of like a family." — Kermit the Frog,
("The Muppet Movie," ITC, 1979)*

Virtually everyone struggles with their finances, whether their cash flow is mountainous or meager. We've seen how the human mind can work against our best financial intentions. In that common ground, we all are "sort of like a family."

I have shared my personal story. Now let me share some stories of people I've had the privilege to meet along the way.

A Realistic Debt Payoff Strategy Breaks the Debt Cycle

Overspending and living beyond his means pushed Chris to chase after more income as a solution to his problems. By not addressing the cause of his overspending, he found that his hard work and sacrifices were in vain.

Setup: One step forward, two steps back

Chris—in his mid-30s and single—wanted to buy a house and start building his wealth. Unfortunately, he was falling farther behind, even after one attempt at breaking the debt cycle.

Two years prior, he'd consolidated $30,000 in credit card debt into a personal loan. At the same time, he felt he was taking another step forward when he changed jobs, getting a raise in the process.

His former employer had offered a 401(k) and Chris took advantage, building some retirement savings. But rather than roll it over to the new company, he thought that chunk of money might help him on his plan to get out of debt. The total only covered a part of his consolidated loan, and he knew there would be some penalty for early distribution of the funds, but he withdrew the money anyway.

Unfortunately, he underestimated that penalty. Left with $25,000, he put $15,000 toward his personal loan, then kept the other $10,000 for himself and for the anticipated taxes for taking the money early.

"I was feeling pretty good then. I figured I was young enough to catch back up with my retirement savings. Plus, I had the new job and a little more income to make that happen. At least, that was the initial plan."

Instead, Chris quickly adapted to the "extra" money in each paycheck. In fact, he decided he should have a new car. He picked a luxury brand with a nice feature package like the top-of-the-line model on the showroom floor. There was really nothing wrong with his "old" car and it wasn't paid off, so he kept it and continued to make the $250 monthly payment.

With the new car, he was fitting an additional $500 car payment into his budget. Without thinking about the difference between the gross amount of his raise and his actual take-home amount following deductions, he had soaked up nearly all the increase from his new job.

With the additional income already spent, Chris started using his credit cards again. Every couple of months, he would see the problem and buckle down with a period of extreme spending cuts and a tightened budget so he could make bigger card payments. But, every time, the amount he would pay was slightly less that the amount he had racked up on his cards.

Over the next year, his credit card debt climbed to about $15,000.

As Chris felt more and more stuck in his debt cycle, he realized that the total he owed now was right back to the level it was before he emptied his 401(k). Only now he had no retirement savings, either.

"I was at rock bottom. I finally knew I needed to make some pretty big changes."

New Situation & Progress: The "make more" fix

Chris thought maybe a side hustle could be one way to start getting out of the hole, so he started driving for an on-demand ride-sharing service. He didn't want to pile up miles on his new car, so he decided that his old car—still with a couple of years of payments left—would be his "work" car. His goal would be to make about $1,000 to $2,000 per month that he could apply toward his debt. Eventually, maybe he could start saving toward a down payment on a home, too.

Not wanting to waste his efforts, he committed to stop using his credit cards and reduce some of his spending.

"I was never big on formal budgets and I wasn't ready to write one up. I always just tracked my spending in my head and figured things out as I went along."

Complications: No better off despite working more

Chris continued with his binge-and-purge spending behavior. For a couple of months, he'd aggressively pay down his credit card debt. Then, after seeing some progress, he'd feel like he could relax for a weekend. That "weekend" turned into a couple of weekends and he would be back to using his credit card. He would justify his credit card usage by looking back at the previous month's large overpayment and consider his current spending to be taking back some of that overpayment.

"In my mental accounting, I was getting ahead. But then I'd get my card statement. I couldn't believe I was actually falling farther behind."

Cutting back again, he'd double down with more driving. After a couple of months, the grind would again take a toll on him. He wanted some fun in his life, too. But without any discretionary dollars in reserve, his only option was to relapse with credit spending.

Final Push: A realistic goal with a realistic solution

Chris realized he needed some new thinking when it came to personal finance. First, he knew only a less-aggressive strategy to accomplish his debt payoff goals would be realistic. Trying to pay everything off in six months was just contrary to human nature. His new goal was to pay off everything in two years. That would still require paying about $1,000 every month, but that was about what he could make with a balance between driving on the side and leaving time to relax and recharge.

A key part of his new plan was to create new bank accounts to route the money directly toward achieving his goals. Driving paychecks were funneled into a new account at the same bank where he had his personal consolidation loan. He'd use that money only toward retiring the loan.

He also broke down his regular paycheck into necessary and discretionary spending. For necessary, regular bills (rent, utilities, car payments, insurance), he set up an account with an auto bill-pay feature so that portion of his income flowed right through to meet those needs. Chris knew his tendency to rationalize and dip into money in his account, so he made sure to block any other access to it. There was no debit card or checks.

He deposited the rest of the money—his discretionary funds—into a third account.

As he tracked his spending more closely, he saw that most of his food spending was on spontaneous purchases and eating out.

"I don't like to cook or buy groceries. That's probably not going to change. So I set a monthly limit that would come from my discretionary account."

With his limits set, Chris identified another $400 that he could set aside toward his goal of paying off debt. He started transferring that to the same side-job account where he had his personal loan. This had essentially become his "goals" account for paying off debt.

Finally, he cut up his credit cards and purposely blocked access to anything other than his discretionary funds. With this setup, he could still do all his budgeting in his head, since he liked mental accounting better than working it out on paper, yet he stopped himself from undermining his efforts.

Aftermath: Freedom from chasing money

It took two years, but Chris achieved his number-one goal of paying off his debt, including the personal loan, credit cards, and car financing.

With no debt, he was able to focus on his primary career and quit his side hustle. An additional benefit of quitting was that he was able to cut back to just one car. Thinking more long-term, he parted with his luxury car and now drives what was his "work car."

He maintains his separate accounts to make it easier to resist spending above his plan. The $400 he had identified as "extra" discretionary income is now split and funneled to an emergency savings account and a "splurge" account. When a need or want to spend comes up—as they always do—Chris doesn't have to use credit.

"I don't drive as a side job anymore. Do I miss the extra few bucks? Maybe once in a while. But the time and freedom gained from not chasing after that income is worth more than the money."

Lessons Learned

- Create a budget you can stick to, with realistic goals and reasonable timelines. Writing it up is best, but if mental accounting can work for you, that's better than nothing at all.
- Making more is perfectly reasonable, but don't get swallowed up "chasing" money.
- Set up your own "Ulysses agreement" by separating and automating accounts to guard against urges for spontaneous decisions that disrupt your plan.
- Consolidating debt can only be an option when you've addressed the underlying problem of spending beyond your means.

Compromising and Prioritizing is the Path to a Sustainable Lifestyle

With the turmoil of change, Kelly's divorce forced her to start over and redesign her financial lifestyle from the ground up. Separating her needs from her wants and prioritizing what was most important to her was the only way forward.

Setup: Recognizing an unsustainable financial lifestyle

Kelly is a 40-year-old, divorced mother of two. She has full custody of her children, but a very good co-parenting relationship with their dad.

She admits to some insecurity about her ability to handle her finances or maintain a budget. During the marriage, her ex-husband controlled the money.

Kelly's $2,000 monthly net income as a part-time receptionist is supplemented with monthly alimony and child support of $3,000. Her flexible hours and four days-a-week schedule enable her to drop off and pick up her kids from school and other activities.

She's also kept the kids in the same schools by renting a house in the district and doesn't want to further upset them with a move. Eight-year-old Ethan and 10-year-old Madison are her priority and she wants to be present and support them through this time of change.

Her biggest piece of the settlement was $150,000 in equity when the couple sold their home. It seemed like a lot at the time, but three years after the divorce Kelly had burned through about half of the money. At that spending level, she was dipping into that money at the rate of about $2,000 a month.

Also included was retirement money from her ex-husband's 401(k) account. So far, she hadn't touched that, but at the rate she was spending the money from the house, she was afraid that she would soon have to.

"One positive is that I haven't borrowed money. I don't even want a credit card because I'm afraid I'll start using it, especially when the kids want something. My biggest goal is to just not run out of money too quickly."

New Situation & Progress: Creating a budget

Kelly is trying to keep life as stable as possible for the kids. But spending above her means, while possible in the short-term, is not sustainable. She could see she was burning through her divorce settlement money faster than she wanted to. Having to find a full-time job or move from her house would further disrupt her kids' school and social lives. Her anxiousness about that and not wanting any more negative impact from the unfortunate breakup of the family moved her to action.

Her first step was to create a budget. She needed to clearly delineate her family's needs versus wants.

Some luxuries from a two-income household were the first to go. No more annual passes for local Southern California theme parks and zoos. It was more than just the cost of the passes. Every visit added spending on gas, parking, and overpriced food.

Entertainment was next. Kelly cancelled her cable service, cutting to internet only. A Netflix subscription and a digital, over-the-air antenna got them plenty of streaming shows and local channels, too.

Her food budget was also a big target. Kelly started making lunches to take to work instead of stopping for quick-serve or at the local grocery store deli. She wanted to plan meals and shop only for food on her list; no more impulse spending. No more membership to the warehouse store either.

"The $1.50 hot dog and soda was cheap, but I never could get out of that place for less than $200."

Complications: Sticking to the budget

Even with the new budget, there still seemed to be "leaks" in the financial bucket.

Kelly still fought the urge toward spontaneous purchases of toys and gifts, especially around birthdays and the holidays. The kids still wanted trendy "fast fashion" clothes that seemed to come in and out of style faster than ever.

Food spending was over budget, too. On days that Kelly worked, she didn't always feel like cooking, so eating at restaurants, or the occasional splurge for take-out or delivery seemed to sneak into the budget. Everyday groceries would add up as well. The kids would raid the pantry or fridge for whatever was fast and easy, and Kelly knew that kind of food was expensive.

Her relationship with her ex-husband sometimes added to her financial stress. She felt that he was always trying to pry into her finances since he knew she hadn't dealt with them before. She didn't want him to know that she was struggling, nor give him the satisfaction of thinking that he was right in controlling the money and keeping her out of the financial loop.

"I wanted to show him we were just fine, even though I knew I wasn't handling it as well as I should have. With me focusing on the kids, juggling work, and making changes, I was getting more and more stressed out, wondering if we could make it. Of course, that just compounded the problems."

The Final Push: Prioritize and compromise to find the best way forward

Kelly was able to take a step back and see what was truly important to her, and what her long-term commitment should be, and it was her kids. What that did not mean was indulging them with everything they wanted and avoiding even the slightest pushback in dealing with them. Not everything the kids wanted was a need. Supplementing her lifestyle with her divorce settlement money or other funds outside her own cash flow was not sustainable. The new commitment meant really finding a way to live within her means.

First, Kelly decided the rental house would not fit her new life. She found a three-bedroom apartment within the same school district. Immediately she cut about $1,000 per month in housing costs from the budget, between reduced rent and utility bills. On the plus side, there was a community pool where the kids and their friends could hang out, and a small gym for her. (She'd been neglecting her own health in keeping the kids happy.)

Fast fashion became a casualty too. The kids could still have some name brands they wanted, but they had to become more strategic in their shopping. Discounters like TJ Maxx and Ross were the new stores of choice. With some of the savings, she was able to also provide herself with a weekly allowance to spend on the inevitable needs that popped up, like gifts, toys or clothes.

Her next target was transportation. First, she sold her big, gas-guzzling SUV. She'd always seen it as part of the "cool mom" package. She was the kids' taxi service and wanted to be the mom that was willing to take the kids and their friends wherever they wanted. She felt it gave her kids an edge socially, too. But it had to stop if she was going to serve her kids' best interests.

In place of the SUV, she bought a four-door sedan that served her needs nearly as well. She not only saved on fuel efficiency but on her overall gas spending because now she was limited in how many other kids she could transport. She found that other parents stopped asking her to drive every time.

With only a handful of changes, she was able to lower her spending to a level where she only needed to tap into her reserves for about $500 each month. At that rate, the $80,000 in home equity money could last well over 10 years, even if it never grew.

"By that time, Ethan will be old enough that I won't have to shuttle him to school and back, and I could probably work full time if I need to."

Aftermath: Maintaining balance

While Kelly isn't adding to savings yet, that's okay. She's living within her means to the point where she no longer has to worry about exhausting her current reserves.

She's fulfilling her priority of taking good care of her kids, too. She can still work part time to be there for them. And she's involved them in her budgeting, too, reviewing it with them every month so they learn the process. Seeing the numbers also helps them better understand what they can and can't afford. She feels less guilty and they have a better perspective on what real needs are, versus what they want or think they need.

There's been an unexpected benefit, also.

"One thing I didn't want to do was go back to court for more support. But since I'm not paying for as many clothes and activities, my ex has voluntarily decided to pitch in for more things. If he wants the kids wearing brand name shoes, he can buy them!"

Lessons Learned

- Redo your budget regularly. The first "cuts" may not be enough, and you'll have to get more serious when it's required to meet your goals. For example, selling the SUV and switching to an economical (more earth-friendly) car.

- Understand your needs versus your wants. Do you really need a house when maybe an apartment might have amenities that give you more bang for the buck?

- Apportion your discretionary income with a weekly allowance to even out your monthly spending.

- Be open to shopping for discounted clothes and other household goods, even non-brand or off-brand items.

- Don't fall for marketing efforts to upsell you bigger, better "stuff." Look for the attributes that cover what you need, not extra features that appear to give more value.

Overwhelming Debt Clouds a Couple's Future

A desire for independence and some bad spending habits had become an overwhelming cloud over their lives. The need for each other's help drew John and Amy closer together, but falling back into old ways pulled them further apart. Instead of dealing with it, they made it worse with a backwards way of managing their credit cards, never addressing the true problem.

Setup: If it's not there, you can't see it

John and Amy had decided early on in their relationship to keep most of their finances separate. They each had successful careers and neither of them really wanted to give up the independence they had become accustomed to. They married a little later than most couples, coming together in their late 30s. By then, they had some entrenched habits when it came to finances and spending beyond their means.

Soon after their marriage, the problem became obvious to both of them, but neither wanted to cut back on their spending. From the outside they looked great, with electronic gadgets, new clothes, cars, expensive vacations, dinners out, and other luxuries befitting a successful couple.

On the inside the problem was growing. They had multiple bank credit cards, plus cards with retailers, too. They opened new ones to gain cash back or airline miles. In one attempt to track spending, they opened new accounts with the plan to use one card each for dining, groceries, gas, or other spending categories. Those plans soon unraveled, with more growing balances.

For a while, they covered up the problem. They each had decent incomes and thought they could always earn their way out from under their debt. Neither of them wanted to make a big deal out of it or tell the other what they should or shouldn't spend their money on.

They were having fun.

"We were just a couple of years into the marriage and we didn't want to spoil that 'honeymoon' phase."

They both tried to respect each other's independence and didn't want to overstep the boundaries they both enjoyed but as the debt added up, they started to look to each other for a little help.

New Situation & Progress: Starting over with debt consolidation

While John and Amy kept separate bank accounts, they both shared their mortgage and household bills. The Southern California home they purchased together just after getting married had appreciated significantly in the short time they owned it.

They needed a quick fix and consolidating their debts into one easy payment felt like a good solution. Since they both benefitted from the appreciation of their home, it seemed like the obvious "joint account" to borrow against.

The couple took out a $75,000 home equity loan and paid off their cars and all their credit cards. They also closed a number of accounts and cut those cards up, never to be used again. It felt like a great step in the right direction. Looking at the consolidated figure also helped them see just how much debt they'd rung up.

They recognized that they needed to be a little more accountable to each other for their individual spending, but still didn't want to give up the freedom of separate spending agendas. Because of the savings from a lower interest rate on the home equity loan, they had improved their cash flow. They agreed to start putting more of their paychecks into a shared household account to cover the increased mortgage payment and not take on any more individual debt. For the next several months they managed their spending together and chipped away at the home equity line.

Complications: Failing to address the real problem

It was less than a year after consolidating their debt that John started using his credit card again without letting Amy know. It started innocently with small purchases here or there as a matter of convenience. A small gift for Amy or something that they both could benefit from justified the use of credit in his mind. He planned to pay it off in a few months and then get back to their plan.

Soon, other more selfish purchases followed. In John's mind, the balance on his card was small relative to the main equity loan. He had a good income and thought maybe a bonus would come his way as in past years so he could get rid of the balance in one payment.

The pattern is a common one. Consolidating debt is a good idea if you address the spending issues. Otherwise, the behavior doesn't change, and the cycle continues.

Keeping the secret from Amy also was a problem. John had no accountability other than to himself. He was finding out the hard way that he needed someone else to help him along the way.

Obviously, Amy could see the new things John had and knew he couldn't be paying cash for them, so it wasn't really a secret.

"It was obvious that he was starting down the same old path, but I was still in 'don't rock the boat' mode. But it really made me angry that he tried to keep it a secret from me. We were supposed to be working on this problem together."

Amy didn't want to be the only one making sacrifices. Rather than take on the issue, Amy also went back to spending.

In time, they both knew what the other was up to. The only strategy they had in regard to their spending was to keep their cards maxed to the limit on purpose. With their credit score downgraded by the large home equity line and their new credit card debt, they couldn't get more cards. The threat of having a purchase declined was the one way they could think of to stop their spending from getting worse.

Compounding the issue, their poor credit score added to the cost of that debt. They were paying 20 percent interest on their "cash back" cards.

The stress on their lives was mounting as well. With little meaningful communication about the problem, their relationship was going downhill. They also were less and less satisfied by buying stuff.

As we learned in Chapter 1, the Hedonic Treadmill has no end and no long-term fulfillment. Instead of fun or joy from the latest purchase, they were feeling guilt and the weight of a lifestyle gone wrong.

Final Push: A third party helps break the cycle

In spite of their lack of control, Amy and John knew that spending so far above their means was unsustainable. The tension in their relationship prevented them from meaningful discussion on the issue, so they agreed to consult with a third party who could help them find a way out.

In looking for someone to help, they were referred to a financial planner by a friend. Wary of a sales pitch, they instead were surprised that the planner started by asking lots of questions about how they had come to this point in their finances.

"That outside perspective is what started our turnaround. You get farther and farther off track and you forget what 'normal' should really feel like. This guy was a voice of sanity for us."

Amy and John also had no idea where to start tackling their debt. The planner had ideas and techniques to get started.

First, he needed the couple to see what they had to work with in terms of income. Starting with a budget, they would know where their money was going and find where they could make changes to free up more money to begin paying down their debt.

Then he asked what was most important to them, both individually and as a couple.

"That was the first time we had really thought about our financial future and our shared responsibility to each other. We had the same goals, we both wanted to be debt free, learn to live within our means, and start meaningful savings, *together*, for our future. That was really the moment we felt like we were on the same team."

They started by paying off their new $10,000 in credit card debt first. The couple had enough income that they never missed payments, but just hadn't been aggressive enough in paying down the balance. With $600 identified from their budget exercise, the credit paydown snowball began. (See Chapter 8.)

Knowing how hard it is for people to radically change habits, the planner offered an 80/20 solution for using the $600. (A bit more aggressive than the 75/25 rule cited in Chapter 8, given the direness of John and Amy's situation.) That way they could still pay cash for some little rewards along the way.

As an additional safeguard against a spending relapse, he also had them call their credit card issuers to reduce the credit limit on their cards as the balances came down.

Aftermath: A big task ahead, but a happier outlook along the way

Having built up over $85,000 in debt, John and Amy have a lot of work to do. Already one card is paid off and the snowball is rolling a little faster on the second one.

The original debt in the home equity line is steadily declining with regular payments as well.

It's true that their lifestyle has changed with a tighter budget. The FedEx truck doesn't come to the house as often as it used to. Amy says it's worth it.

"You find that *stuff* just doesn't make life what it should be. Working on this problem together may not seem like fun, but we feel so much better now. Talking about this problem makes it easier to talk about everything. We've kind of rediscovered each other and why we got together in the first place. Believe it or not, this is way more fun than when we just did whatever we wanted."

Lessons Learned

- John and Amy went for a quick fix instead of addressing the spending habits that got them into trouble in the first place. That won't fix the underlying problem.

- Achieving common goals takes teamwork and if you share your finances with a partner or spouse it is important to work together. Even if you keep your finances separate, you can still be accountable toward common goals with honest and open communication.

- Have a plan for what you want to accomplish. A third party can bring ideas to the table on how to solve a problem and be a good accountability partner if you need a little outside assistance.

A Young Couple Begins to Make Changes for the Future

Michelle and her husband Andrew are a typical young couple, and their financial story is typical too. They've reached a point of frustration because their income has increased significantly, but they're just not making progress financially. Recently they have begun setting goals and taking a few first steps toward financial freedom.

Setup: A move to Southern California brings opportunity, but adds debt

Both from the Midwest, Michelle and Andrew married in 2013 and had kids right away. Little by little each month, they began accumulating credit card debt.

The couple moved from the Midwest to Southern California in early 2016 and received a significant pay increase. Thinking they would have a lot more money to spend, they didn't realize how much higher the cost of living is in Southern California. For example, their rent jumped from $800 to $2,500 a month. Utilities like electricity for air conditioning, and water for their lawn, came at a premium, and easily added another $400 to their monthly expenses during the summer.

Between the cost of the move and adjusting to a bigger lifestyle they ended up adding $10,000 in credit card debt despite the pay raise for a grand total of close to $25,000.

Early on in their marriage, the couple made a simple mistake by getting forbearances (a suspension of payments) on Andrew's student loans, which were approximately $75,000. The idea was to pay more on their consumer debt before tackling the student loans. Unfortunately, with forbearance, though the payments are on hold, the loans kept accruing interest. This made their loan payments even higher.

Michelle was the one to do the budgeting and pay the bills. Her efforts to handle the bills came from a desire to not burden Andrew with it.

"He's an operations manager and handles the finances of the company. He doesn't want to come home and deal with money or make sure household bills are paid on time."

New Situation & Progress: More opportunity than ever

Even though the move came with a higher cost of living and more debt, they still felt like they were ahead of the game.

After only a little more than a year with his new employer, her husband was offered a partnership in the new company along with three pay raises, tripling their income to about $150,000 per year. There was more room for advancement, too, something Michelle said was not going to happen without the move. Andrew felt he was never going to move up in his job in the Midwest.

He was given a company car to use for work, so they decided to trade in both of their old cars for a single vehicle. That decision came with an additional $12,000 loan for a new minivan.

Complications: With increasing income comes an increasing desire to spend

The main struggle for Michelle was that, as they made more she wanted to spend more. Even though pay increases were supposed to go toward debt, when the money hit their bank account her thoughts returned to: "What can we spend this 'extra' money on?"

They continued to ratchet up spending to meet their increasing income. Michelle recognized that she had a "spender" personality and that her mindset was not an easy one to change. Michelle tried tracking all of their spending, but it seemed like little expenses were slipping through the cracks and they couldn't really see where their money was going. Michelle always felt like they were in paycheck-to-paycheck mode.

They tried a financial workshop through their church and felt like they failed miserably. Michelle said she wasn't willing to buy into a system that meant "suffering" until they were debt-free. Drastic lifestyle cuts were not something she was willing to do. She did not want to cut out vacations, dining out, or other leisure activities even if that meant it took more time to tackle their problems.

"I'm willing to make smaller changes, but not be miserable."

Their financial issues became relationship issues for Michelle and Andrew and, for her, money fights are the worst fights to have.

"We just look at money differently, I want to enjoy the money and if I have the money, why not spend it. He's better at fighting the urge."

Final Push: A new budget and a new plan emerge

Michelle and Andrew recognized that they needed a change and it needed to start with getting on the same page. Michelle wanted a clear picture of where they were spending, but knew that tracking expenses was always a struggle.

"Before I could make a budget I needed to understand where our money was going."

Rather than tracking their expenses on their own, they used a free app and online tool through mint.com to track their spending for them. Once they identified where their money was going, they asked themselves where they wanted their resources to go.

In previous attempts they recognized they never really bought into their shared vision for where they wanted to be.

"We knew we wanted to be debt free, but we never really had a vision for why."

They both wanted to get out of the paycheck-to-paycheck cycle and stop feeling the stress of living beyond their means. They also knew that without any emergency savings every unexpected expense went on a credit card.

They also spent time exploring why so much of their money was going towards the expenses their mint.com account was showing them. Restaurants and dining out was eating up more than they wanted it to, but getting to the root of that uncovered a desire for convenience.

"After a long day of work or chasing after a three and five-year-old, neither of us wanted to cook, let alone clean up the mess."

Michelle and Andrew found that they could prepare multiple meals on the weekends and either reheat them or do minimal cooking to be ready to eat. As an unintended benefit, Andrew was able to take lunch to work more often and cut fast food almost entirely from his diet and their budget.

By focusing more on eating meals at home the budget shifted to groceries instead of restaurants, but again most of their food expenses revolved around convenience.

Michelle tried using coupons or shopping for bargains, but didn't like the burden of "strategic shopping." Both Michelle and Andrew needed motivation to seek out cost savings because if they were left to purchase groceries in the moment, they would never look for deals.

By limiting the amount they could spend on groceries each month, they were more focused on stretching every dollar and finding a way to get the most food within the set limit of grocery dollars.

"It became a game between me and Andrew to see who could get the most food."

One budgeting trick picked up from the financial workshop was envelope budgeting. The problem they had with that system was that they would keep borrowing money from one envelope to spend in a different category and the whole thing would fall apart.

Michelle started participating in a gift-card scrip program through her church. She buys gift cards to the places where she plans on spending money and a small percentage goes back to the church.

There are plenty of options with the gift cards, too. She can get them for gas, groceries, restaurants, and retail stores, and in several different denominations.

The gift card program essentially mimics the envelope budgeting system (see Chapter 7) or using cash only. The gift card takes the place of cash in an envelope that you can spend only for that budget item.

While Michelle and Andrew have identified several goals, at the top of the list is becoming debt free. Michelle is quick to point out, however, that debt free doesn't include the student loans—at least for now. They know those loans will take many years to pay off.

Here are their goals for now:

- Live below their means and maintain a margin between income and spending.
- Build some emergency savings over the next 6 months. They realize that an unexpected expense could end up going on a credit card. Michelle knows that would be counterproductive to their first goal and doesn't want to lose momentum.
- Retire their credit card and auto loan debt in two years.

"At this point, we aren't thinking much about retirement. When the credit cards and auto loan are paid off—hopefully in the next two years—we will re-evaluate and see what we can do to tackle the student loans."

Lessons learned

- Motivation to change comes from understanding *why* you want to change. Consider what is most important to you when setting your goals.
- While tracking every expense can be tedious and stressful, knowing where your money is going can help you reevaluate priorities and allocate money to the areas of your budget that are most important to you. Leverage free apps or websites to help. Your bank likely offers some helpful tools as well.

Aftermath: On the same page

Michelle and Andrew see areas in which there's temptation to spend more, like moving to a bigger rental house or getting a second car. But they are focused on making smart decisions and stretching their dollars as far as possible. Their behavior is changing for the better and Michelle is much more aware of her habits and is paying more attention to prices. She never used to buy off-brand items; Andrew swears there's no difference. Giving in to that change is enabling them to save more money.

Their budgeting has uncovered about $800 a month and any bonuses or unexpected extra money has gone toward paying down debt. Even though it means they don't get to splurge and enjoy spending that money on themselves, they enjoy the feeling of accomplishment that comes with paying off large portions of debt.

These steps are alleviating some stress, too. Like relationship stress.

"Just acknowledging these issues cuts the tension. We're working together now, rather than against each other like we were. We're on the same page."

Life's Inevitable Twists and Turns Can Upset the Best of Plans

Will has always kept an eye on his future self. His story includes a number of fairly significant life changes—both good and bad—that never turned his financial world upside down, but forced a financial reset at a late stage in life. Despite a few substantial setbacks, he found contentment in a more sustainable lifestyle.

Setup: Life upends the dream

Like most boys, Will dreamed of being a professional athlete. Ice hockey was his sport of choice. With some talent and a few breaks, he beat the odds and made it to the American Hockey League at age 24, just one step from the sport's highest level, the National Hockey League.

Soon after, a dose of reality hit. At 25, he was released. (Actually, he was offered a few minor league deals. But young and prideful, he rejected that option.) A year later, he reconsidered and tried a comeback, but ultimately the sport had passed him by. He had no more dream job and no idea what his next career move would be.

Fortunately, during his minor league days, he had worked during his off-seasons. He wasn't a spender, so he had a financial cushion that gave him time to figure things out.

New Situations & Progress: Another bump in the road, then steps up the ladder

In time, his professional hockey connections led Will to a marketing agency. Soon he was married and at age 27 became a homeowner, again using earnings saved, which had grown through investments.

Another temporary setback hit when the agency closed. But within six months he was hired as a sports reporter for a local newspaper. At age 29, he made an annual wage of $20,000 and became a new dad.

But even in the late '80s, Will could tell that journalism was not going to be a path to making more than "survival" wages. At age 31, he quit the reporting job and returned to marketing, this time in high-tech, which was in full-growth mode at the time. The move immediately increased his salary by 30 percent.

A second child arrived in 1990. Will worked several side gigs, earning up to $7,000 extra per year. Annual raises moved him up to about $50,000 annually by 1995.

Eventually, Will could see that his employer was not heading in a good direction. He pursued an escape strategy, lining up two half-time clients, then quitting his full-time job to become a marketing consultant. The decision was not popular with his wife, who questioned whether he could make it work. It was understandable with his young family.

"It was the best decision I ever made. I was right about my former company, which within a year imploded and was sold off in pieces. And within six months, both of my clients offered me full-time jobs. I chose the company that would become my work home for the next two decades. They brought me on with a $10,000 raise over my former job."

Around 2000, Will was blessed with two sizeable inheritances—over $150,000 in all. The timing of the first taught him a valuable lesson in preparation for the second.

With the dot-com boom in full swing, he started investing in the stock market. It seemed every stock he picked was a winner. Overconfidence led to more investing. When the bubble burst in 2002, he estimates he probably lost about 60 percent of the initial $50,000 inheritance.

Will was more conservative with the second, putting it into money market funds. The higher interest rates at the time paid several hundred dollars per quarter. Those funds provided some nice discretionary cash for the couple.

More changes were ahead. In 2000, his company moved him from Irvine, California to Charlotte, North Carolina. Will and his wife sold their first house for about twice what they'd bought it for. They found the Charlotte suburbs remarkably affordable compared to California, and bought a 3,800-square-foot home with a walkout basement on half an acre for $240,000. They could have paid cash, but they decided to take out a small mortgage.

"All our moving expenses were paid by my employer, plus I was paid moving bonuses worth tens of thousands. I was making six figures, had all that extra cash, and still had the 'fun money' checks coming every quarter. Times were good."

Complications: The first taste of more than enough

Will felt that his time in Charlotte was the tipping point when he and his wife felt the tug to get on the bigger-better train.

"Our neighbors were all in climbing mode, constantly seeking more money, better cars, and bigger houses. Charlotte was booming. My spouse didn't need to work and she did a lot of shopping with all that extra time."

"When we moved, we had plenty of people telling us to ditch our cars and just buy new ones when we got to Charlotte. So we did, and not just what we needed, but what we wanted to match up with our new friends."

They finished the basement, bought new furniture for their new home, and ate out a lot. More money was soaked up by a family trip to Disney World, side trips to Washington, DC, and Florida, and a hockey tour with the kids to see several NHL cities. They never price-shopped, just buying what they wanted.

Will knew they could have been making better use of all that "extra" money.

"We paid cash most of the time, but I could have put a lot more away for retirement, or real estate, or something more long-term."

After only a couple years, his company moved him back to Irvine. Again, the company paid all moving expenses. And, even in an overbuilt Charlotte real estate market, Will managed to make a profit on the sale of their home. However, with all the improvements they'd made to the house, the gain was small.

The Irvine real estate market, on the other hand, had kept growing rapidly. They had to use the equity from their first two homes and most of the second inheritance to buy a home for $500,000 in their old neighborhood.

"It needed a lot of work—new carpet and tile, plumbing fixes, a couple DIY projects to redo the paint and landscaping, and a bathroom remodel. With our moving bonuses gone and no more income from the inheritances, we had to keep it pretty conservative."

In the next few years, the infamous housing market bubble took off. At one time, Will's new Irvine house was valued at about $900,000. All around them they watched neighbors show up in big new SUVs and pay for extravagant kitchen and backyard remodels. Fortunately, he could sense that was a bad idea.

Also, Will had known since the move to Charlotte that his marriage was headed nowhere. That also kept his urge to spend in check. Will could see the end coming and the inevitable divorce came when Will was 54.

"Of course, marriage is about love, respect, and trust, but mine was ultimately a mistake and it turned out to be the biggest blow to my financial future ever. Though my divorce was probably as civil and inexpensive as they come, when you add up all the losses in income, retirement, home equity, and opportunity cost of how that money might have grown, it probably set me back over a half-million dollars."

For Will, the changes weren't done yet. In 2016, after nearly 21 years at the same company, Will lost his job at age 59. He was earning in the mid-$100,000s, including stock and cash bonuses, with salary increases every year. Then they decided he wasn't a fit.

"Even though I never had a negative review and had just received an increase the previous year, the employer had the final say—'at will' they call it. All it took was a new person in management who wanted to push me out. And, frankly, with that management change, the work was not satisfying or fun anymore."

The final push: New choices for the years ahead

These were supposed to be his high-earning years, and Will wasn't ready to fully retire. The reality was that at 59, Will could get a similar job, but it probably would pay quite a bit less. He didn't want to start over with another full-time corporate job.

Taking a new look at his finances, Will had to prioritize what he needed and how he could achieve his goal of being self-employed. Unfortunately, the obvious first requirement was to downsize out of his home. He loved the house and neighborhood, and didn't want to leave it, but it was clearly a time to "prioritize and compromise."

A severance payment from his old employer, plus the house sale and proceeds, helped him make a final settlement to stop paying alimony, cut his expenses, and semi-retire. It wasn't going to be the retirement of his dreams, but he would be able to maintain a comfortable lifestyle.

"I'm living what they call the 'portfolio life.' I do a few different things to keep some money flowing in, but I don't have to work the daily grind. Though I do have to pay attention to prices now!"

Lessons learned

- Think about swallowing your pride if it means having a job versus unemployment. Your position doesn't define you and you're more attractive to employers when you have a job.
- Be mindful of how inheritances are comingled with household finances, and seek professional guidance if you have concerns about how an inheritance may be divided up in the event your marriage dissolves.
- There will be high-earning years when you're tempted to spend more, but you can still be content during those years if you funnel more money to long-term goals.
- Preparing for a job loss is the reality of today's job market. You may think you're safe in your job, but you can easily be just one management decision away from being let go.

Aftermath

Here's what Will's life looks like now, despite losing the substantial cash flow from his former job:

- No mortgage.
- No debt.
- Six-figure 401(k) rollover and investment accounts.

- Residual cash from home sale.
- Consultant work to supplement, but no necessity for another full-time, high-paying, high-stress job.

"I'm thankful for most of the choices I made. There were a few crossroads where I might have taken on financial obligations that would have bound me to work full time now. Instead, I chose to save the money and give away a lot of it. That's not to boast, but just to tell you that it is infinitely more satisfying to see that money help people who need it, rather than seeing something like a luxury car sit depreciating in your garage. In the end, it's just a car. I got hit with some life-changing events, but came out just fine."

These stories might seem relatable, or even familiar. You may have felt the desire to make just a little bit more to get caught up or get ahead. Maybe you've struggled with living beyond your means and you understand the consequences of carrying debt. You may have experienced the difficulties of shared finances with a spouse or partner and struggled to stay on the same page.

Whatever your story, there is a solution. You can rewrite your script and live the life you want. You can create financial freedom by living within your means.

When you first think about living within your means, it's natural to think that you are reducing your fun and fulfillment. But are you really that easily pleased?

Would we rather use credit to buy something now and feed a system rigged against us? Do we need to consume today at the expense of our future? Do we need to exchange time for money, chasing after more income to improve our lifestyle? Do we need to spend every dime we make—and more—to build our self-esteem by keeping up with the Joneses, putting our financial stability in jeopardy?

I don't think so.

Instead, I hope you get the feeling that building the discretionary margin between what you earn and what you spend creates an exciting opportunity for you. Now you can take control of your lifestyle, focus on what is most important to you, and spend your money in more meaningful ways.

By moving step-by-step through these pages, I hope you've paused to see the bigger picture of what you truly want for your life. I hope that you see the benefits of reduced stress—financial and otherwise—on your overall well-being.

I encourage you to implement the tools and strategies from this book to build new habits and to spend more wisely. Prioritize your needs, wants, and financial goals and build a plan that allows you to achieve the lifestyle you want. Now go, rewrite your story, accomplish your balancing act, and create financial freedom.

Appendix: Resources

The resources listed here are presented for your information only. Listings here do not imply any endorsement or recommendation by Dave Baldwin.

Budgeting/Spending Apps and Software

- Balancing Act Documents – www.thebalancingactbook.com

- 10 Free Household Budget Spreadsheets For 2018: christianpf.com/10-free-household-budget-spreadsheets/

- CountAbout – Browser-based app: countabout.com

- Intuit Quicken – Software for installing on PC or Mac: quicken.com

- Intuit Mint – Free ad-supported app: mint.com

- MoneyDance – Personal finance app for Mac: moneydance.com

- Mvelopes – Electronic envelope budgeting: mvelopes.com

- You Need a Budget (YNAB) – Advice and software: youneedabudget.com

Saving and Investing Apps

- Acorns – Purchase tracking and investing: acorns.com

- Digit – Automated savings: digit.co

- Personal Capital – Personal financial planning: personalcapital.com

- Rize – Automated savings: rizemoney.com

- Trim – Automate ways to save: asktrim.com

- Truebill – Finds recurring subscriptions, bank fees: truebill.com

- Couponing – The 20 Best Coupon Sites (Updated for 2018): moneypantry.com/best-coupon-sites/

Minimalism

- The Minimalists – Book, blog, podcast, documentary on using it as a tool to find freedom: theminimalists.com

- Becoming Minimalist – Pursue your passion by owning fewer possessions: becomingminimalist.com

Personal Finance Books

- *Dollars And Sense: How We Misthink Money and How to Spend Smarter*, Dan Ariely & Jeff Kreisler, HarperCollins Publishers, 2017

- *End Financial Stress Now: Immediate Steps You Can Take to Improve Your Financial Outlook*, Emily Guy Birken, Adams Media, 2017

- *Live Your Life for Half the Price*, Mary Hunt, Revell, 2015

- *Your Money or Your Life*, Vicki Robin, Penguin Books, 2008

- *More Than Enough: The 10 Keys to Changing Your Financial Destiny*, Dave Ramsey, Penguin Books, 1999

- *Misbehaving: The Making of Behavioral Economics*, Richard Thaler, W.W. Norton & Company, 2015

- *Nudge: Improving Decisions About Health, Wealth, and Happiness*, Richard H. Thaler, Caas R. Sunstein, Penguin Books, 2009

- *Predictably Irrational: The Hidden Forces That Shape Our Decisions*, Dan Ariely, Harper Perennial, 2008

- *Teaching Kids to Buy Stocks: Stories and Lessons for Grown-ups*, J.J. Wenrich, Hopeful Hill Press, 2019

- *The Automatic Millionaire: A Powerful One-Step Plan to Live and Finish Rich*, David Bach, Crown Business, 2016

- *The Cure for Money Madness: Break Your Bad Money Habits, Live Without Financial Stress — and Make More Money*, Spencer Sherman, Broadway Books, 2009

- *The Cheapskate Next Door: The Surprising Secrets of Americans Living Happily Below Their Means*, Jeff Yeager, Broadway Books, 2010

- *The Millionaire Next Door*, Thomas J. Stanley, Ph.D, RosettaBooks, 2010

- *The Rational Optimist: How Prosperity Evolves*, Matt Ridley, HarperCollins Publishers, 2010

- *The Richest Man in Babylon*, George S. Clason, Reprint Edition, Dauphin Publications Inc., 2015

- *The Ultimate Financial Plan: Balancing Your Money and Life*, Jim Stovall & Tim Maurer, John Wiley & Sons, 2011